DEDICATION

This work is dedicated to Garrin Benfield. Without your enlightened forgiveness, this project would not have been possible. Also, special thanks go to my friends in San Francisco, my cohort at CIIS, and to Benjamin Tong. To the Benfields -- thanks for your support and encouragement all along the way. To my parents and family, thanks for the lifetime of experiences that have given me the eyes to see so many of the things that found their way into this paper. And, finally, to all of the patients who have shown incredible bravery in opening up their inner world to me so that I might share their narratives: thank you!

TABLE OF CONTENTS

DISSOCIATION AND ITS DISCONTENTS:

AN EXPLORATION OF THE ROLE OF DISSOCIATION

IN A RETRAUMATIZATION CYCLE

AMONG VICTIMS OF REPEATED TRAUMA

ABSTRACT

Dissociation is a key defensive strategy employed by developing and developed psyches in the face of terrifying events. These events, known as traumata, can leave a vulnerable ego with little recourse but to create a perceived safe haven deep within the psyche where one might hide from a threatening person or environment. This place of solace then becomes a habitual escape from a hostile world when the ego feels threatened.

As time passes and the child continues to develop, the child who fears the worst of the world and its inhabitants is at a disadvantage, unable to face its challenges head on due to fear that one is not up to the task; and so there is retreat. This pattern of retreat prevents the ego and all of its varied components from starting anew and objectively perceiving any others as existentially separate from the self or even from perceiving distinct self-states within the self. Instead, one responds to all objects as if they were the original introjected object as if they are actually a part of him or her.

And so the child is in repose, frozen deep within the self. These missed cues set the stage for an imposing drama defined by a pattern of protective defenses beginning with the safety-seeking routine of dissociation, passing through stages of projection and projective identification, re-introjection, and commencing in a grand finale of re-traumatization that leaves him or her once again convinced of the terror that defines the epic tragedy that is life.

Using lenses provided by trauma theory, Psychoanalytic study, and Neuropsychology this dissertation will examine the role that dissociation plays in keeping a person not merely a victim of past trauma but one who lives in a constant battle with the elements that more often than not, get the best of the person each time.

CHAPTER I: INTRODUCTION

Trauma and its sequela are perhaps the most threatening series of events that the human personality could endure on its shaky and ever-shifting journey from its early days of pure contact-seeking infancy through its frightening and sometimes terrifying bad object introjections. Like a fragile vessel being torn asunder under the weight and power of a sometimes-perfect storm, the developing ego experiences trauma in the dark of night with no harbor to cradle it safely in the midst of a swelling sea nor a shaft of light to guide it along its path. If a "good enough" caregiver is not found, the ego heads into the bow of the ship, hoping to stay warm and dry while Poseidon rages above.

Creating the tenuous illusion of a safe place, the ego, paralyzed in terror, hides from a force for which it is no match, hoping it will soon pass and the light of day will return. If the environment into which the developing person is born continues to provide a milieu which is experienced as threatening, he will continually return to that semi-protected space, deep within his psyche, creating a pattern that will endure into adulthood.

This continual withdrawal away from the outside world and into the interior, isolated passageways of the psyche can cause the child to eventually miss any and all cues that the environment has changed, that he can now return to the deck and face the weather as it is now and not what it once was. In missing this change, the traumatized soul sets himself up to experience every environment and everyone in it as terrifying. He will prop up his defenses both in retreat and in battle until the vicious cycle is repeated and again he retreats to his safe place, awaiting the next storm.

How then does the traumatized individual find himself unable to see dry land over the swells that keep his boat on a constant state of near collapse? Sigmund Freud postulated a "repetition compulsion" (Freud and Gay, 1989), which may indeed offer some insight into a description of events as witnessed from the outside. Still, he offered little explanation of "how" this process occurs and under what circumstances.

Later theorists like Sullivan (1937, 1953, 1954, 1956), Fairbairn (1952, 1954), and Winnicott (1960, 1964) began to speculate that instincts and drives could not explain how injurious problematic relationships can be (Mitchell and Black, 1995).

Expanding on the suggestions by Melanie Klein that infants begin to organize their world (and their egos) at the mother's breast and possibly before (Likierman, 2001), a dramatic shift began to occur that set the stage for a conversation about the power of early relationships (and the often unconscious meaning they tend to carry) to create pathological relational expectancies that would endure into adulthood.

As clinical psychologists, we encounter pathologically-organized individuals whose inner and relational worlds are filled with frightening characters and experiences. For many, the fear of the world and its inhabitants is so powerful and ubiquitous that an entire personality structure is built around regulating (and avoiding) the anxiety that is provoked by simple acts in day to day living. This is a frightening proposition for those who live in such worlds and a frustrating endeavor for those of us trying to treat them.

This paper makes an attempt to deepen our understanding of the particular mechanisms involved in developing and maintaining the dissociative processes that appear be involved in keeping those who are repeatedly traumatized from actualizing a life that has been liberated from the insults that were suffered early on. The cycle of retraumatization is obviously a complicated, multi-stage process and describing each step in detail is beyond the scope of this work. With that in mind, some effort will be made to describe the "macro-processes" involved in retraumatization like dissociation, projection, projective identification and re-introjection. The bulk of the work will involve examining the defense of dissociation and its short-term prophylactic effects along with its dangerous, long-term consequences when it is employed as a primary mechanism in the process of affect regulation.

With this in mind, our research questions are presented to us. How does a victim of repeated trauma come to utilize dissociation as a primary method of affect regulation? How does dissociation set a person up for re-traumatization? And, finally how does dissociation prevent a person from moving beyond the re-enactment of a traumatic past and into a life of first-hand experiences in the present?

This paper will largely utilize the language and descriptive capacities created by psychoanalytic literature in general and from Object Relations Theory (Fairbairn, 1952, 1994), (Winnicott, 1960, 1964, 1965, 1969, 1988), (Guntrip, 1961, 1967, 1971, 2001) Trauma Theory (Herman, 1987, 1992), (Levine, 1997) and Inter-

Subjective/Relational Analysis Theory (Benjamin, 1990),

(Bromberg, 1993, 2000, 2003), (Davies and Frawley, 1991),

Mitchell, 1988), (Mitchell and Black, 1995), (Stern, 1983, 1995,

2003, 2004), (Stolorow, 1992, 1994, 2001) in particular. It is

assumed that modern, inter-subjective models of personality

development have eclipsed classical analytic thought and therefore

will form the major theoretical underpinnings of this study.

Additionally, relevant literature from the neighboring discipline of

neuropsychology will be considered in order to add quantitative

support for the findings.

The goal of this study is to examine existing literature in the

aforementioned fields in order to identify common themes as

described by prominent researchers and theorists in theoretical

orientations that include but are not limited to Melanie Klein, (Klein

1930, 1932, 1935, 1952a*, 1952b, 1996; Likierman, 2001) Fairbairn

(Fairbairn 1952, 1994; Pereira and Scharff, 2002), Sullivan, (Evans,

1996; Sullivan 1937, 1953, 1954, 1956), Guntrip, (1961, 1967, 1971,

2001), Winnicott, (1960, 1964, 1965, 1969, 1988), Bromberg,

(1993, 1995, 2003, 2004) Stern, (1983, 1995, 2003, 2004), Jessica

Benjamin, (1990) Hirsch, (1995, 1997), Fromm, (1964), Judith

Herman, (Herman, 1992; Herman and Van der Kolk, 1997), and Peter Levine (1997). The authors considered in this study were selected (a) because of the explanatory power of their writings for descriptive narratives of the human experience, (b) their recognition as authoritative voices in their respective disciplines, and (c) the power of their observations to offer insight into the topic at hand in this paper.

On occasion, I will use case material from my own psychotherapeutic work. While any and all of the cases that I consider were part of my clinical work as a doctoral candidate and none of the cases will have been involved in true psychoanalytic therapy, they will still be offered as illustrative of conceptual and theoretical considerations that come up as this paper is presented. No suggestion will be offered that case material is an exact representation of a concept under consideration but an attempt will be made to describe how it is that I believe that a case narrative exemplifies a given subject.

While making a theoretical exploration of a complicated process such as dissociation is a challenging task, it is worth considering the bulk of the literature on the subject as a whole, as the authors presented here have, crafted a body of theoretical and conceptual knowledge base that is in need of a critical review. Along with my own clinical experience, I looked to the accepted writings for clues into a process that has been described from multiple perspectives and synthesizing a common, explanatory narrative is the research methodology best suited to begin to address the research questions that were outlined earlier (Newell, 2001).

Individuals who have been repeatedly traumatized often find their lives to be defined by frightening experiences for which there are often few explanations. Patients with Borderline (and other) Personality Disorders, Dissociative Identity Disorder and Post Traumatic Stress Disorder (American Psychiatric Association [DSM-IV-TR], 2000), and other disorders involved with affect regulation and relational difficulties are commonly seen in clinical psychology. Adult men and women who were once victimized by a dysfunctional family or a pathological individual are now unable to escape their frightening pasts as they find themselves living day to day in the aftermath of their trauma as it is maintained as a current event rather than as a relic of the past.

Clinicians are often known to express frustrations with those who were once thought to be "un-analyzable" and who are now often referred to as "difficult patients". These are the hurting souls who have come to be victimized by personality organizations that leave no room for the personal and emotional growth that accompanies new and rewarding experiences for those not so ordered. By linking the observations of established theorists, it is a goal of this paper to offer some aid to these victims by promoting a better comprehension of the processes involved.

Understanding the process involved in the maintenance of trauma as a going concern is a key responsibility of those of us in clinical psychology and neighboring fields. It is hoped that this study will help to expand the descriptive and explanatory power that we have to offer our patients. When they seek help, our ability to offer therapeutic intervention is always hindered by our individual and collective limitations in understanding their experience and always enhanced by greater knowledge of their presenting issues. This paper intends to expand our knowledge and understanding of these psychological processes that are the source of pain for so many.

CHAPTER II. REVIEW OF LITERATURE

A Project's Genesis: The Retraumatization Cycle

Our belief is that the interpretive process within the analytic

experience is the only way to end the constant cycle of

dissociation, projection, projective identification,

reintrojection and retraumatization that makes the history of

abuse not only a painful memory, but an ongoing reality

(Davies and Frawley, 1991, p. 294)

This dissertation in general and this literature review in

particular owe much to the work of Jody Messler Davies and Mary

Gail Frawley. Theirs was a rich description of a cycle of

retraumatization as it appeared in a 1991 article titled "Dissociative

Processes and Transference-Countertransference Paradigms in the

Psychoanalytically Oriented Treatment of Adult Survivors of

Childhood Sexual Abuse" (Davies and Frawley, 1991). While the

process of inquiry that this paper has inspired to endeavor within has

changed my understanding of dissociation (and each of the other

terms in their retraumatization cycle as defined) the seed was planted

upon my first reading of this seminal work. In many ways, I owe a debt for my interest in the topic of trauma in general and in dissociation in particular to this team of remarkable writers.

Writing largely about the treatment of victims of sexual abuse, this article has many implications for the psychotherapeutic work that is done with trauma victims and we will return to this theme later in this paper when we begin to consider the impact of a relational understanding of dissociation on clinical work. For now, it is their nuanced and richly conceived understanding of the process of dissociation as a protective mechanism for the ego and a coherent sense of self for the victim that will draw our attention.

Distinguishing dissociation from repression, which is likened to defending against unwanted drives, Davies and Frawley open up their article with the suggestion that dissociation is a process that is key to (while appearing structural in nature) the larger operational style of a person that we might think of as personality (Davies and Frawley, 1991). "We use the concept of dissociation to refer to an organization of mind, not unlike splitting, wherein traumatic memories are split off from associative accessibility to the remainder of conscious thought, but rather than being repressed and forgotten, as would be the case in a topographical/structural model, they alternate in a mutually exclusive pattern with other conscious ego states" (p. 6).

The memories of abuse are not locked away in a trunk in the back of the minds attic, they are actively kept out of consciousness from the person as she traverses from affective state to affective state (Davies and Frawley, 1991). The purpose, of this dissociative process, according to the authors, is to separate the ego or "self" from the internalized object world that was created in relationship to essential, caregiving objects who were neglectful, abusive and worse. Through unconscious process, she is protecting the core of her sense of self from the behavior of the original objects who perpetrated the first trauma.

In reference to the "ego states" that Davies and Frawley detail, it appears that they are talking about "different experiences of consciousness" (Davies and Frawley, 1991, p. 276). These transient states, common to us all, are split off from one another in traumatized individuals, inaccessible to conscious process as they would be in someone whose ego did not develop these dissociative patterns as a result of trauma. Further, a return to the dissociative pattern of the repetitive shifting between and within these states is triggered over and over again by interpersonal relating, inadvertent access to glimpses of memory and the overall emotional state of the traumatized individual.

Specific to the sexual abuse victims (which we are taking here as analogous to victims of trauma), Davies and Frawley suggest, that through a process of enactment within the psychoanalytic dyad (and elsewhere in their interpersonal life), traumatized people often vacillate between those self-states that can be thought of as suggestive of the abused child and those that can be suggestive of the now fully grown adult (Davies and Frawley, 1991). While there are other permutations of these states and others, the focus is on the enactment of these states within the field and the potential to work with them.

If, as the authors suggest, the dissociation process acts as a barrier between these ego state enactments, then the trained therapist must not objectively interpret those states from an outside perspective as the material to be accessed, emotionally experienced and understood are unavailable to the "intellect" in the constant matrix of shifting states (Davies and Frawley, 1991). It is only by entering these dissociative states, hand in hand with the client by allowing the enactments to safely occur that the information can be bought to consciousness and then worked with. While the clinical implications are obvious, the theoretical suggestions are worth making explicit as well.

In the model suggested by Davies and Frawley, an active process is constantly keeping the traumatized individual in the dark (Davies and Frawley, 1991). Ever unaware of the process of shifting and the information attached to the states being shifted away from, she is perpetually trapped in a cycle of misinformation about his experience. This misinformation is key to the understanding the process of retraumatization. Without access to the traumatic and frightening experience of his past trauma and to the process that keeps him from experiencing it, a powerful unconscious mechanism is operating below the surface, doing it's insidious work. And ultimately, setting up the person for projection of his great unconscious anxieties on to those who happen to trigger him.

The Davies and Frawley article is a profound and insightful piece of literature that asks us to consider several important themes if we are to understand the powerful consequences of trauma on an adult survivor. While there are multiple details that could be more thoroughly studied in other works, for the purposes of this paper, we will focus on the processes of dissociation and it's relationship to enactment, projection, projective identification and re-introjection that contribute to the maintenance of trauma as a part of the present and future of traumatized individuals rather than as a disturbing artifact of the past.

Shift From a Drive-based, Structural Model Toward an Object Relations Theory of Personality

From its inception, the field of clinical psychology has been preoccupied with healing trauma. Seeking to provide a measure of relief to "hysterical" patients, Sigmund Freud set out to create a model of personality development that left room for error, namely the potential for emotional illness as injury (Freud, 1989). For Freud (and for most of us who have followed in his footsteps), the evidence that difficulties experienced during the maturation process could have potentially painful consequences was painfully obvious.

Freud's model of personality was a structural one whose development was fueled by instinctual drives for survival, procreation and even death (Freud, 1989). Under this paradigm, an infant was only half person, and the other half animal. Civilizing influences were needed in order to turn this raging infant in the crib into a functional person who was capable of long-term relationships with other tame humans. For Freud, instinct was behind all manner of pathology. Relationships served to mitigate those instincts.

This drive theory may have held explanatory power for a world attempting to make sense of the revolutionary-but-dehumanizing theories published by the famed evolutionist Charles Darwin (Darwin, 2003) and for sorting out the senseless violence of World War I, it ultimately lacked the descriptive capacity needed to create a broad understanding of the human experience that would account for relational trauma.

Freud Versus Janet

It should be noted that it is not simply future writers separated by years of interpretive distortions of Freud's writing who resisted the notion of a structural understanding of the unconscious and its implications for the warding off of unwanted material from conscious awareness (Freud, 1989). In Freud's own time, a noted rift had already formed between Pierre Janet and himself on the notion of dissociative processes versus repression as underlying the primary blinding processes of the unconscious (Kihlstrom and Hoyt, 1990).

Freud was under the assumption (and he adamantly defended this) that the expulsion of unwanted material from consciousness was a voluntary process endeavored upon by the patient willingly (Singer, 1990). Freud's understanding does make sense when one thinks of the process of storing mental experience as static and even structural in nature. If the mind is composed of literal spaces where memories are stored, one can choose to ignore or simply avoid consciously accessing that location.

Within a more modern understanding (and perhaps better informed with more recent empirical support) of a model of consciousness that places greater emphasis on the mind as facilitative of various inter-related processes than on location-oriented storage faculty, it becomes a greater challenge to accept his model of repression. If there is no central location responsible for the storage of events and various experiences, how then can one voluntarily avoid that location?

Janet on the other hand, suggested that repression was the consequence of limitations in the quantity of synthetic capacity of pathologically structured individuals (Singer, 1990). While this appears to be in line with a model of dissociation that is undergirded with an eye toward avoidance of psychic overload (which is closer to the stance that this paper takes) there are limitations to this understanding as well. Freud was under the impression that all humans have the capacity to "repress" and Janet appeared to suggest that the process was pathological in nature and thereby nearly absent in healthy individuals.

Perhaps both had some measure of truth in their arguments. It appears that the capacity for denial of experience is a normal (and all too common) phenomenon that we likely take for granted in even the healthiest of psyches. It seems also true that there are pathologically oriented individuals that seem to "dissociate" as a matter of course, as if their innate capacity for tolerating affective stimuli were somehow diminished.

Neither theorist however, was able to quell the argument entirely and for some time, the happy medium seems to have been to accept that they were talking about separate processes, with Freud suggesting repression and Janet suggesting dissociation, or desagregation as he termed it. Time, however, seems to have been on Janet's side in some respects as an affect-regulation) and thus much more process-oriented) understanding of the avoidance of certain mental phenomena appears to have more critical favor as the years have passed.

Melanie Klein and The Infant Psyche

While Freud considered repression to be a consequence of the anxiety experienced as a child while he was having his instincts tamed out of them by potentially threatening adults (Freud, 1989), Melanie Klein noticed that children appeared to be attributing threatening characteristics to the adults in their lives through a process of fantasy that had less to do with intentions behind the behavior of the actual adults and more to do with their perceptual experience of that behavior (Klein, 1952).

This conceptualization of infants and children as having a fantasy relationship with their caregivers was a major advancement in analytic thinking. If children were attempting to make sense of their relationships through confirmatory processes rather than directly as the consequence of their behavior, the inner world of children and their imaginings of relationships had begun much earlier than had previously been thought, and were more directly related to a child's innate ability to connect with and attach meaning to the outside world than simply to react to the behavior of a condemning caregiver or even society.

While Melanie Klein never abandoned a drive theory in her formal writings (Mitchell and Black, 1995), by looking closely at what she has written about her observations of the inner life of infants, we find that the foundation for a relational theory of personality can be identified. For Klein's infants, the world was a black and white experience divided between the realms of pleasure and pain (Klein, 1935). A hungry infant was a frightened infant and in that frightened state of mind, the infant is imagined as attempting to make sense of the absence of the breast. Was it her fault? Had she destroyed her life-sustaining object? Was the breast a threatening object who sought to destroy her? In this process of sorting through her anxiety and joy, paranoia, depression and ecstasy, the child begins to create the forms, pattern and expectancies that will define her relational life which will likely last into adulthood.

The Schizoid Experience

In this sometimes frightening world of "objects" children are thought to be creating dynamic maps of relationships and of the people and "things" in those relationships. Whether the world would become understood as a welcoming place full of safety and nurturance would depend, in part, on the child's ability to successfully navigate between her states of mind and the fantasies attached to those states. A child who is overwhelmed by her anxiety may come to fear the world and continue to use primitive defenses to protect herself from the destructive elements in it and may find herself unable to reconcile her anxiety. A child who is able to process her experience and identify the world as a safe place, is likely to mature in her appreciation of others in it as mostly safe and helpful (Klein, 1996).

Attempting to shift away entirely from the drive-model of personality, the British school of analysts led by Winnicott, (1960, 1964, 1965, 1969, 1988) Fairbairn, (!952, 1994) and Guntrip, (1961, 1967, 1971, 2001), began to imagine that drive theory actually accounted for little of human personality development and began to develop a framework around a purely relational model of development. For Winnicott, the sole job of the primary caregiver was to provide the necessary emotional and nutritional conditions that would enable a child to mature and develop in an appropriate and healthy way (Winnicott, 1960).

For Fairbairn, an infant began to make sense of the "objects" in his life as soon as he had the capacity to do so. Fueled by a "libidinal ego process" that provoked a desire to connect with the outside world, the infant began the process of determining the valance of the outer world and in turn, the child's inner world would take shape. In this view, the inner world of a child was, like Klein's, a fantastic place full of symbols that were imagined as either frightening or benign depending on how the child experienced the object.

A frightening "other" would be "introjected" as a thing to be feared and would provoke a similar fear reaction whenever it was encountered in the future (Guntrip, 1971). This was Fairbairn's "bad object". These frightening objects would cause the child's ego to split off, turning inward to avoid the anxiety. This "schizoid withdrawal" into a place the child could feel safe would form the basis of a pathological self-other relationship to the outside world and others in it (Guntrip, 1966).

An object that was experienced as safe and pleasurable would confirm the child's belief that the world was also safe would contribute to the development of a healthy self. A child whose libidinal energy continued to encourage him to encounter his world with optimism would be thus prepared to experience healthy relationships as life progressed (Guntrip, 2001). If there were any schizoid withdrawal (and he maintained that there always was) it would be minimal and managed through mature defenses. These children, with a supportive template of human relationships in place, would be pre-destined to experience happy (or at least benign) relationships with the object world.

As time passed and the shift in psychodynamic thinking from a drive-based/instinct and structural model of personality began to be supplanted by a relational/libidinal and process-oriented one, psychoanalytic process also began to shift (Mitchell and Black, 1995). Observation in the clinical setting had always been a major method employed in the theoretical construction of new ideas as the field shifted ever forward, encapsulating new concepts that were being validated through experience and thus forcing the abandonment of those that no longer appeared relevant or were apparently contradictory of both experience and empirical study.

This progress would continue into the modern era as thinkers like Stern, (1983, 1995, 2003, 2004), Bromberg, (1993, 2000, 2003),

Mitchell, (Davies and Frawley, 1991; Greenberg and Mitchell, 1983;

Mitchell, 1988; MItchell and Black, 1995), Aron (Davies and

Frawley, 1991), and others would begin to combine Sullivan's

interpersonal/analytic theory (Evans, 1996; Sullivan, 1937, 1953,

1964, 1956), which is essentially a relational model of personality

development, with an affect regulation-oriented perspective to create

an inter-subjective paradigm that would transform theoretical and

clinical thinking in powerful and unexpected ways. In fact, it would

be a revolution.

Harry Stack Sullivan and Interpersonal Analysis

Writing in the 1920s, Harry Stack Sullivan's writing feels

more prophetic than historic. Today, the interpersonal field is a well-

established theoretical assumption with many of the brightest minds

in the analytic community describing the phenomena associated with

an interpersonal perspective with great clarity (Mitchell and Aron,

1990). Steven Mitchell, Donnel Stern, Philip Bromberg and others

currently on the vanguard of analytic thinking to varying degrees

accept a model that emphasizes a mutual creation of perceptual reality and personality over one that is based on a static self who merely encounters others in object form (Stolorow, Atwood, Branchaft, 1994).

Working with patients with very serious mental health issues (namely schizophrenics), Sullivan rejected the idea that individuals have a single personality that is expressed in a singular entity created against a backdrop of drives and instincts as Freud had largely postulated (Mitchell and Black, 1995). Instead, Sullivan noticed that his patients who had been regarded as unable to connect with anyone, were indeed able to connect with him. Sullivan believed that his patients were able to express different components of themselves to different people and that in fact, it was the relationship between two people that would influence their ability to connect with the other (Sullivan, 1953).

While Sullivan was never a developmental theorist (Mitchell and Black, 1995), he did establish some principles associated with childhood experience that would begin to offer descriptions of potential early life experiences that shape personality. For Sullivan, this process largely involved the management of anxiety (Sullivan, 1953). He proposed that a young infant generally floats between periods of relative contentment and periods of anxiety. When the child was fed and sated, the infant was relaxed and at peace. When the infant was uncomfortable, hungry or missing the caregiver, he was anxious.

Sullivan suggested that these anxious states had a distancing effect between the mother and the infant as their relationship with one another was based on an interpersonal experience that exchanged affects back and forth between them (Sullivan, 1953). This symbiotic relationship was potentially a source of anxiety to the infant as these affective colorations were contagious. If the mother was anxious, the infant too would become anxious and vice versa, creating an unpleasant distancing between the two as the infant would not be fully able to allow the mother to move in to soothe him as she was the very source of her anxiety.

This anxiety is distinct of fear experiences which have a more "integrating tendency" between mother and child (Sullivan,

1956). Over time, the infant begins to create a model of a "good mother" who soothes the natural tensions of hunger, discomfort and loneliness with relative ease and a "bad mother" who reacts to the child's tension by becoming anxious herself or based on her own personality and temperament, bring her own anxiety to the relationship, making the child more anxious (Evans, 1996, p. 82).

Using the good mother and bad mother as examples, the child begins to internalize and associate the mother's self states within this symbiotic relationship as "good me" or "bad me", setting her up for a potential lifetime of anxiety management around these acquired "self states" (Sullivan, 1956). If anxiety is sensed, the infant shifts toward behavior that is associated with a "good me" that calms the mother (and herself).

Managing these states, is Sullivan's "self system" which he believed was finely attuned to managing anxiety (Sullivan, 1954). Using the term "security operations", Sullivan suggested that an infant's desire to reduce anxiety is a natural tendency just as are "needs for satisfaction" (Sullivan, 1937). When this management system senses anxiety, security operations emerge and attempt to reduce the anxiety that has been sensed. When that tension has been reduced, the infant then feels safe and secure enough to pursue her need for satisfaction. Over time, this system becomes perfected, in fact unconscious. Sullivan referred to a well-functioning self-system as "suave" (Sullivan, 1956).

This self system develops in relationship and is repeated throughout life in relationship. For Sullivan, the "self system" and its management of anxiety (and the good or bad "self states" associated with it) is at the center of personality (Sullivan, 1956). In this way a personality can be thought of as a creation of the infants formative experiences with the care-givers. In this model, anxiety (and the personality attached to it) is not a function of an infant struggling to tame anti-social instincts in a conformity-demanding world, it is the result of a constant inter-subjective experience with others. There is no self without the other.

Within this model, Sullivan also created a place for dissociation as a defense to emerge. He postulated that in experiences where the infant experiences extreme anxiety, an amnesia occurs regarding the behavior just before the incident (Sullivan, 1956). Instead of "good me" or "bad me", the incident effectively becomes "not me" (Evans, 1996, p. 86). For the infant who is exposed to extreme anxiety for which there is potentially no remedy, the infant has no ability to create a self system that can reduce the anxiety or provide satisfaction. For these infants, experiences are felt as random or dissociated.

Over time, these traumatized infants can potentially be imagined as "wired" to dissociate from anxiety (which may ultimately become generalized) of any kind. These "unformulated experiences" (Stern, 1995) are Sullivan's hallmark contribution to the role that dissociation plays in retraumatization. In these "self states" that in fact are not fully formulated in the infant's mind, few new experiences are possible, in fact they are precluded. If the infant is missing important clues on how to react to anxiety, the stage is set for a dramatic process that ultimately ends in the person re-experiencing the trauma and accompanying anxiety that is at the heart of the problem in the first place.

One can see from this point of view that, if this model holds, there are very serious consequences to this method of anxiety and overall affect management. While the dissociative processes may in fact allow the infant (and later adult) to reduce short-term anxiety by "checking out" and placing the experience in a "not me" category, the story does not end there. How then will the infant learn to develop relationships with others who are not the frightening and anxious "bad mother"? Will not she be re-traumatized over and over again each time the self system senses this generalized anxiety?

What seems to be the case here is that the devil we know is better than the devil we do not know. In essence, the person caught in this trap is consistently choosing to reduce the powerful unconscious anxiety that was provoked early in life when the infant had no power to change her circumstances in exchange for more common anxieties that may be manageable through cogitation or other processes. The example that comes to mind here is of the patient who constantly complains that all of the women in his life drive him crazy by nagging him about his lack of ability to be emotionally intimate while making no connection to the possibility that the mother he has described as "neurotic and controlling" may have created the initial anxiety which he was too small to have done anything about.

Harry Stack Sullivan contributes prominently to this work. His emphasis on relationship, the self system and anxiety reduction were written at a time when Freud's drive-based model was not only in vogue but was the mainstay of analytic thinking. Many years later, the analytic community would revisit Sullivan's work to help establish an inter-subjective model of personality development and to potentially provide descriptions of dissociative processes that result in people living their current lives defined by past trauma with little possibility for escape without great risk to the perceived sense of self (Mitchell and Black, 1995).

Klein Shifts Toward a Relational Model

Once a shift away from a drive-based model where objects are mere accidents of discovery in a process of discharge (Mitchell and Black, 1995) is complete and a theoretical framework is established whereby the world of internal object relations becomes the centerpiece of a model of personality development, new consequences and logical questions arise.

While Melanie Klein held firmly to the notion that she was merely extrapolating on Freud's point of view, others weren't so sure this was true and a subsequent reading of her theoretical writing point squarely in the direction of (and lead directly to the development of) an object relations theory (Mitchell and Black, 1995). Her protests aside, we shall consider her writings themselves and put her theoretical contributions in the context of an object relations theory.

Melanie Klein studied infants and children. She was committed to the idea that they could be analyzed and believed that their play could and should be interpreted the same way as an adult's patients dreams, parapraxes and free associations should be (Klein,

1932). It should be carefully noted that a great deal of interpreting was done that could not be directly confirmed or denied by the infant's themselves. To be sure, we don't know exactly what the fantasy life of the infant looks like or exactly how they interpret those fantasies. With this in mind, we must closely evaluate behavioral correlates used to support theoretical assumptions as well as consider the adult narratives of childhood experience in thoughtful and systematic ways.

Based on her experiences with children, Klein put forth several major contributions to the psychoanalytic literature that maintain resonance and persuasive power to this day (Mitchell and Black, 1995). Of them, Klein's descriptions of the "paranoid-schizoid" position vs. the depressive position seems most relevant to describe here as we consider the history and development of dissociation within a relational/trauma and affect/regulation theory of a re-traumatization cycle.

Klein perceived the infant's relationship with the mother as an ambivalent one. At times, the infant perceived the mother's breast as a comforting object which provided physical comfort, relief of distressing hunger and a source of calm emotional connection (Klein, 1952b). One can easily imagine a contented infant, eyes closed, suckling quietly, uttering gentle sighs of relief as his anxiety slowly drifts into the past. This breast, in the infant's mind, is associated with a positive affective state that likely generates joyful reverie in the mind of the still-developing infant. While the child's cognitive abilities lag, what is lacked in descriptive and explanatory power is made up for in phantasmagorical relationship defined by self-state experiences (Mitchell and Black, 1995).

On the other hand, what the lord (or mom) giveth, the lord taketh away. If indeed the child is satiated by a full and flowing breast, he must also have experienced a hunger that leads to a need for satiation (Klein, 1952). Klein's infants experienced hunger as caused by an absent breast as a painful, anxiety producing experience that would have the infant locked in frightening imaginings of annihilation and a subsequent retaliatory desire. Fear and anger would taint the fantasies that the infant experienced and the good breast once thought to be such a source of love and goodness, was now a mortal foe. This threatening object was not yet reconcilable to the loving object and the child found himself in a position of living in a highly emotionally valanced world that was often difficult to predict.

For Klein, the infant was trapped. A fear of death and destruction followed by not-yet-understood destructive urges to destroy the object that also provided nourishment and comfort were the underpinnings of the "Paranoid-Schizoid" position (Klein, 1952). By using the term paranoid, Klein was referring to the fear associated with his own death and/or the potential destruction of the good breasts and schizoid as a reference to the "vigorous separation of the of the loving, and loved good breast from the hating and hated bad breast" (Mitchell and Black, 1995, p. 96), otherwise known as the defense of splitting.

Defined as one position, one can easily imagine an infant whose cognitive capacity to get him out of this jam (as a confused child) and lacking any clear understanding of these two contradictory experiences: love and hate. Here, we spot what might be considered the beginnings of Klein's contributions to an affect-regulation and inter-subjective perspective on emotional trauma. If the infant cannot learn to reconcile his two highly stimulating objects, how will he be able to relate to a world that is both pleasurable and painful?

How will he love those who hurt him? The schoolyard is a tense place with bullies and sweethearts, tears and joy, and a school-aged child who has yet to remedy this problem seems doomed from this vantage point. Forever unable to trust that the world will not be his demise and forever condemned to retreat to manic splitting attempts in order to find some temporary relief. Would all who encounter this troubled soul be doomed to be projected upon as completely evil or completely good or both? In fact, Klein herself suggested that the primary struggle in life was in managing fear and aggression as a consequence of the anxiety provoked during these formative years (Klein, 1935).

Fortunately, while according to Klein all children experience the paranoid-schizoid position as a self-state experience during infancy, a maturational process facilitated by an intuitive and capable care-giver can help provide an alternative to the panicked tone of the position (Klein, 1952a). Here, Klein pointed to another tendency that she believed was inherent in the human experience: integration-oriented operations.

For Klein, the infant experience of retaliatory rage toward the mother would lead the child to an intense remorse of his own destructive power. If he, being a supremely powerful master of his own world, were to act on his rage and kill the bad object, would not the good object die as well? Whether or not this conundrum is logically extrapolated by the developing personality is not clear but we know that Klein believed that remorse created by the fear of destroying the good object sets the stage for a reconciliation of the split objects into a whole that is neither entirely bad nor good (Klein, 1952b). This is what Klein describes the "depressive position".

The depressive position, from this vantage point seems unfortunately named. Could it not also be considered the maturational position? Or even the reconciliation position? While consequences of the position may be more developmentally sophisticated than the paranoid-schizoid position, it should be stated that Klein believed that the experience of the child was emotionally depressive due to the remorse experienced by the child for his fantasy of destroying the very thing he loved (Klein, 1935). With this in mind, considering the felt experience of the subject at hand, the use of the term depressive position becomes increasingly appropriate.

It should be noted here that Klein felt an explanation for the depressive condition came out of an instinct-based model that more closely resembled Freud's approach than an object relations-oriented explanation. She believed that the balance of the libidinal instinct versus the death instinct were behind this tendency to reconcile the objects (Klein, 1968). The child, dependent in a very real sense, had a vested interest in survival and therefore must find a reason not to destroy the good object for that would destroy the self as well. Later theorists would explain this reconciliation in relational terms and that will be taken up at a later point in this work.

Object Relations: Fairbairn, Winnicott and Guntrip

As we continue down the path from Freud's powerful, initial (if incomplete) observations of human experience to a modern, inter-subjective theory of personality (and the pathology associated with it that will lead us to understand the role that dissociation plays in the process), it is clear from this vista point that the shift from man as a purely pleasure seeking thing to a relationship seeking one is a necessary one. If man is simply here to gratify himself, why then would he continue to form relationships at all? Why not simply cut himself off, rape the land and anything else he needs that stands between him and his desires?

Klein, being a dedicated student of Freud's, did not answer this question. She remained committed to the notion that the human's primary drives were matters of life and death. Still for Klein, her infant was not simply an animal to be tamed by the socializing effects of the mother and society at large. The infant was "driven" to attach to the breast as a matter of course, as if her life depended on it (Klein, 1952a).

While it is difficult to imagine how Klein reconciled this apparent object-seeking model of development (one where survival depends on attachment to the mother rather than simple pleasure fulfillment) it is worth noting that by simply pushing back the relational attempts of a child to connect from the oedipal phase in Freud's model to infancy (and possibly before), she forever altered the psychoanalytic landscape and her observations created the foundation for the building of a pure object relations theory (Mitchell and Black, 1995). Additionally, by suggesting that internal object representations were "a natural and inevitable feature of mental life" (p. 91), we are at least challenged to investigate and understand how infants (and we as adults) learn to understand and relate to those object representations and the objects they represent.

The infant-mother dyad, a stimulating visual metaphor if there ever was one, underlies all object relations theorists attempts to explain human development. Once Klein began to describe the importance of the mother's relationship with the child (beyond merely feeding him and keeping him alive) others began to make the case that the process of attachment to the mother is a survival mechanism and in fact all infant needs begin and end with the mother due to their utter dependence on her.

William Fairbairn, possibly the most important figure in object relations theory, makes the case that the object of libidinal drive is not pleasure but it is the object itself (Fairbairn, 1994). For Fairbairn, the child is wired to attach and connect to the mother for survival, for personality development and for ego development. And, these early patterns of attachment to the mother set the stage for a life-long relational drama whereby the child, as he develops through adulthood, seeks to attach to others using these early interactions as a template.

Fairbairn studied abused children and was most impressed with how strongly children seemed to attach to parents even when these parents did not provide needed affection or pleasure (Mitchell and Black, 1995). In fact, many of the interactions between the caregivers and the children were painful endeavors that provoked anxiety within the child. Still, they attached. In fact, these children came to seek pain as a part of their connection to others, preferring it to more gentle and soothing interactions (Guntrip, 1961). Here, Fairbairn provides an explanation to Freud's vexing "repetition compulsion".

In Freud's model, it is not clear why a person would continue to make their own lives miserable. In Fairbairn's we see children who are prone to connection at all costs, this is their reason for being and without it, they do not exist (Guntrip, 1971). With this in mind, we no longer wonder why adults in our practices seem to continue to marry the wrong people, expose themselves to relationships that objectively seem doomed to failure and generally recreate painful emotional entanglements. They have no choice. To connect to others is life and if the only way they learned to connect to others is a source of pain, then without intervention, this is the only model they have.

Fairbairn departs from Klein in an important way at this juncture. For Klein, the mother's job was help the child soothe after experiences with frightening objects of which the infant was unable to make sense (Klein, 1930). For Fairbairn, the libidinal drive was outward by nature and was generally satisfied by connection with others (Guntrip, 1971). In this way, the child could maintain a relationship directly from the object itself and derive satisfaction from those encounters. It is only when a frightening or unsatisfying interaction with an object occurs that an object becomes internalized as a representation or "introjected".

For the child who has parents who are not able to meet his needs, or worse, frighten him, the child cannot reach those parents and then creates an internalized version of them that she is able to reach (Guntrip, 1973). Here, in this internalized world of object representations, the infant now has the parents inside of him or put another way, a part of him. Fairbairn believed that there was no need for a child to do this with satisfying objects since they were available to him in the real world and thus there was no need to compensate for the lack ability to attach to them (Fairbairn, 1994).

These internalized object representations become the primary mechanism whereby projection becomes a part of later relationships. For the person struggling with the "bad object representations", they inevitably get in the way of him being able to relate to others in novel (and truly successful) ways (Guntrip, 1971). As a person begins each new relationship, the ego is unable to perceive the other as truly other, a new being separate from himself. No, the other is confused with the internalized object representations that she carries (that she has carried since infancy) and she relates to this other as she relates to this "other" within herself, in a desperate groping way, fueled at once by a libidinal drive to connect but thwarted by an anti-libidinal process that prevents her from making contact just as she was unable to do in infancy (Pereira and Scharff, 2002).

While Klein saw object representations as essential, Fairbairn saw them as necessary evils. Philosophically speaking, a question arises at this point. Within Fairbairn's theoretical framework, is it possible to have a world made purely of objects? Must we all

introject and create object representations due to the inevitability of

"bad object relations"? What would someone who had no introjected

object representations look like? Possibly there is no answer to this

question but it is worth asking them if only to ponder the logical

consistency of the object relations system.

While we may keep hope alive that somewhere out there that

there is a person who is capable of pure object relations without

being encumbered by the internalized object representations she

keeps within her, it is helpful here to understand Fairbairn's

understanding of how the system works. For Fairbairn, the libidinal

drive to connect with others never fully goes away (Guntrip, 1973).

After all, it is essential to survival. In this model, the ego, as it

encounters frustrating encounters with others, splits into distinct

components. One component is the part of the self which continually

attempts to connect to the actual objects (parents) in the outside

world and the other is part of the self that is directed inward, toward the represented objects with whom she frustratingly attempts to connect (Pereira and Scharff, 2002).

One consequence of this process that inevitably frustrates the developing child is that in order to connect with these internalized parents, she must absorb their way of being. She must identify with them (Guntrip, 1973). One can easily imagine how a vicious cycle might take hold in this system that leaves the person with the proposition of living with emotionally challenging relationships with others throughout his life.

This continual desire to connect (fueled by a libidinal ego process that always desires to connect to the parents for satisfying interactions) is continually frustrated by an anti-libidinal process that is identified with the frustrating and denying parents. This likely serves two purposes. On one hand it keeps the ego from fully investing itself into new object relating attempts due to the pain and frustration experienced by earlier attempts to connect. And, on the other, it keeps the person in touch with the hurtful parents with whom she necessarily had to identify with in order to feel attached to. One finds herself in a painful predicament.

Here we see Fairbairn's attempt to explain why it is that people seem to continue to make their lives more frustrating by getting involved in unhealthy relationships. Without help, if they do not continue to identify with the internalized object representations of their primary caregivers, then they may feel as if they do not exist at all (Guntrip, 1971). The power of a desire to connect with our primary caregivers is so overwhelming that it overrides attempts by the libidinal ego process to connect anew, with new consequences.

A final complication created by Fairbairn's theory is that we are largely unaware of these processes. Just as we fall in love for reasons that we do not understand, so it is that we connect with others who hurt us for reasons that we do not understand. This dissociation of processes, according to Fairbairn, serves a purpose. If we were to be fully aware of the dangerous qualities of our internalized object representations, then we would risk losing them and we have already explored the consequences of that in this work.

The splitting of these processes inevitably results in the creation of "discontinuous self-organizations" (Mitchell and Black, 1995, p. 121) that are dissociated from one another. These dissociated self states are what I believe lend some answers to the question of how dissociation maintains a system whereby individuals are continually traumatized by their past in their present lives.

Harlow, his Monkeys and A Need to Connect for Successful Survival as Evidence for Object Relations-based Model of Personality Development

While Freud may have helped us to see that the human condition is marked by inner, psychodynamic conflicts that lurk below the surface of consciousness, constantly bubbling up into the adult world, signaling innumerable adult pathologies, his explanation for them may have been incomplete. At the time of his writing, the physiological understanding of evolution was limited to physical survival. For him and many thinkers of his day (who were still reacting from Darwin's revolutionary studies), the human and his brain were adapted merely for survival (Mitchell, 1988). At the time, it was thought that our increased cognitive abilities were the result of increased survival mechanisms. Only later, once this increased capacity was established was the development of culture made possible.

While our brains and bodies most certainly did develop as an aid for our survival, later thinkers began to conceive of the notion that the picture was broader and more dynamic. It was beginning to be thought that our ability to socialize and interact with others was not simply a result of increased brain capacity but perhaps a cause of it, or at least a co-evolving factor. As noted anthropologist Clifford Geertz notes "It is not that the human brain came first and then culture, or rather man's capacity for culture emanated from it; and this carries the additional implication that the human brain could not effectively function outside of culture, that it would not work very well if indeed it would work at all". (Mitchell, 1988, p. 18).

What was beginning to emerge was the notion that man's survival is not merely facilitated by food and sex. The old adage that "man cannot live on bread alone" is most appropriate here as we begin to realize that it is his ability to relate and therefore to interact successfully with others that allows him that capacity to survive. The human brain did not evolve on the African savannah alone, in isolation, but in concert with his fellow man (Mitchell, 1988). This profound shift in understanding is not simply a matter of words. If one is to accept that man is hard-wired to connect with others in order to guarantee his survival, then his most primitive drives and instincts no longer are simply the result of a need to procreate, they revolve around the need to connect.

Supporting this new hypothesis, evidence for an interactional theory was beginning to accumulate. "Today, we know that within moments after birth, the human voice is the "auditory stimulus most likely to capture the infant's attention" (Mitchell, 1988, p. 23). Implied here is that even in the gestational period, the human is learning to respond to the voices outside of the womb. While it is impossible to tell if this is an inborn instinct or the result of early womb experiences, what can be inferred is that as soon as the infant begins to experience the world, he is beginning to interact with it.

Additionally, research supports the idea that human babies are also drawn to the human face. Studies of infants in the delivery room have shown that they have a preference for the human face even before the child had seen one (Goren, in Mitchell, 1988). Additionally, a human baby's eyes fixate and converge at a distance of eight inches from his own face, approximately the distance from the mother's face from a suckling child. If this child were merely programmed to nourish his body physically, one would expect him to focus on the immediate object of his nutrition: the breast. Instead, we see a baby naturally positioned to look directly at the human providing that sustenance.

Furthering the human/animal understanding of the need for early emotional attachment to the parent figure was Harry Harlow. In his experiments, he learned the hard way that the infant monkey is indeed in need of love and connection. When Harlow placed his subjects in "total isolation for the first eights months of life, denying them contact with other infants or with any type of surrogate mother," they were permanently damaged. Additional experiments documented that the young simians preferred and were more relationally successful in their early lives when they were placed with a wire monkey coated in soft fur than simply being fed by a wire surrogate (Harlow, 1959). If the baby monkey merely needed to survive, sufficient warmth and a bottle should have done the trick.

With this in mind, it becomes much easier to understand why early interactional experiences with the caregiver are so powerful and have such lasting effects. In the frightening and stressful early environments of youth, connecting to others is a powerful indicator of the potential for survival. While undoubtedly, some infants may be born without such relational capacities, this is not a reason to overlook the usefulness of them. In fact the intense instincts of the mother to care for weak or frail infants seems to support the hypothesis that they too are programmed to care.

This caring is present from the beginning. What appears to be the case is that mother and child are in tune with one another from the earliest moments. While later research has asserted the presence of oxytocin and other empathy-inducing hormones, Tustin notes of the emotional interactions between them: "processed by a caring recipient in a sane and practical way, the experience can begin to flow back to the child in a transformed and bearable form so that it begins to process for itself" (Tustin, 1981 in Klein 1987, p. 88). The child is understood here as gleaning his very sense of self and others in these interactions.

If we assume that the need to be loved and that the need to love (interact and relate) are indeed a major component of our capacity to survive, the groundwork is laid that these early experiences are likely to have lingering consequences on adult psychology. If, from the earliest moments, the child is learning its abilities to relate and attach to others, these memories are surely affect laden (Siegel, 1999). It is reasonable to conclude that these pre-conscious memories are likely to be lingering under the surface just as Freud thought that his drivers for survival were.

Winnicott and The Mother Infant Dyad:

As we explore the role of dissociation in a traumatization cycle and we trace it's conceptual and theoretical development over time, perhaps Donald Winnicott more than any other theorist provided insight into the experience of the infant and the mother. Winnicott was first a pediatrician and then an analyst and his writing about the mother-infant dyad reflects a combination of both fields. Winnicott believed that an infant must have a stable subjective experience in her early life if she is to develop a sense of herself as "a distinct and creative center of her own experience" (Winnicott, 1965). The role of the mother was to provide that experience.

Winnicott believed that the process began before the infant was born, during the last stage of pregnancy.

In the womb, the fetus grows to such an extent that it begins to crowd the mother's internal organs, affect her diet and just about every part of her routine (Winnicott, 1964). During this process, the mother learns to shift away from her subjective experience and begins to learn to become finely attuned to her unborn child and her experience. This is helpful (and even evolutionarily beneficial) to the infant because during her formative years, he must come to see the world as a benign place where he gradually becomes aware of himself as a human who has the power to influence her external world. The mother creates a worry free "holding environment" where the child's needs are anticipated and satisfied and leaves him with a sense of confidence about life .

During this time, Winnicott believed that the child existed in a kind of reverie that he considered an unintegrated drift of consciousness, and out of that space comes spontaneous wishes, feelings and desires like hunger and discomfort (Winnicott, 1988). It is the mother's responsibility to provide those desired objects in a nearly seamless fashion so that a natural feeling of omnipotence begins to emerge within the child's developing psyche. This omnipotence is a natural consequence of "good enough mothering" and is the foundation upon which the infant will construct its paradigm for relating to the outside world, in fact, the paradigm of his very sense of self (Winnicott, 1964).

The object relations school in general and Winnicott in particular clearly place a great deal of emphasis on the role of the mother in helping the infant slowly become a person with a gradually developing sense of self and the means to use that self in interactions with the outside world.

For Klein, the infant who was properly soothed by the mother successfully navigated his way through the depressive position in order to merge good and bad objects in one, better understood integrated object (Mitchell and Black, 1995). For Fairbairn it was a sense that a well cared-for child could relate to external objects with minimal confusion of those external objects with his internalized object representations (1952). Bridging the gap, it seems to be Winnicott who suggests that successful navigation of the infant and childhood phases involves avoiding most anxiety associated with the outside world with the aid of a good mother who creates a pattern of relating to the "other" that imbues a sense of confidence in the infant (1964).

The temporary surrendering of the mother's needs as she communes with the infant creates an inter-subjective experience between the two that determines the valence of later object relations (Winnicott, 1964). The infant is not merely alone in the world attempting to make sense of frightening sensations and images. Nor is he reaching out to the world blindly, attaching to the first thing that comes along. The infant is, from the very beginning of consciousness, locked in an inter-subjective space that will be the first in many inter-subjective relations where his various self-states are brought into being. This first relationship becomes a template upon which one's self emerges but the relationship that will encompass many of the infants' self incarnations and his ability to allow his sense of omnipotence to flourish will determine his ability

to confidently integrate those self states without bumping into

Fairbairn's internalized object representations (Fairbairn, 1952).

At its heart, this paper is concerned with dissociation. So,

then the question emerges. What happens if there is no "good

enough mother?" Winnicott believed that an infant who is

prematurely forced to deal with a world of desires and demands due

to his mother's inability or unwillingness to intuitively meet those

demands, becomes "impinged" (Winnicott, 1964). In his model,

impingement refers to the ceasing of the development of the child's

healthy sense of self. In a sense his development is interrupted and

prematurely, he must develop a self who can handle these

challenges.

This "false self" or "split self" as Winnicott would term it is

the consequence of this early shift into the adult world of self

reliance (Winnicott, 1969). The child is no longer able to stay

absorbed in his subjective experience, feeling his omnipotence and

building his confidence. As a result, his developing ego splits within his own self leaving a "true" self which holds real desire and meaning in the world and a "false" or "compliant" self which is forged out of a pragmatic need to deal with an impinging world.

Klein (1987), Fairbairn (1952) and Winnicott (1960), three of the formative thinkers in the development of an object relations based theory of personality all point to the power of a caregiver to set a young child up for success or for failure. In each instance, the infant needs his primary caregiver to impart a template for interacting with the outside world. Occasional failure may result in anxiety, some difficulty with object relating; perhaps of the kind we are all familiar with. Frequent or perpetual failing by the caregiver results in trauma; the kind of repeated trauma that this paper has as its focus.

The infant who is neglected, abused or even used to satisfy a mother's needs rather than his own is left on his own. The inter-subjective bliss is destroyed and the infant no longer feels safe and secure in the dyad. And, if the arms of mother are not safe, then it is unlikely that a preverbal infant will find much else in the world safe either. When this happens, an infant must find a way to cope, to find some relief from oppressive anxiety. Splitting seems to be at the heart of an infant's process.

"If I can keep the good and the bad separate, I may not be destroyed" might be a way to verbalize this unverbalizable and frightening experience. Is this an early precursor to dissociation as defense? If premature self reliance causes the ego to unconsciously split off parts of itself into self-states that are relatively protected from the anxieties of the other, does this set the stage for dissociation later in life to encourage retraumatization? Does the split ego dissociate in order to keep self states separate? If the ego splits and these self states can no longer access one another? These are the many questions at the center of this inquiry.

Interpersonal Trauma Theory

Judith Herman -- The self as it is formed in relationship

and the Potential for Trauma to Shatter

While Judith Herman is not a developmental theorist, her work in the field of trauma has much to say about the impact of repeated psychological insults on children. In her definitive work on the subject *Trauma and Recovery,* (1992), Herman devotes several chapters to the effects of repeated trauma on young people. Here, Herman contrasts the ideal human developmental outcomes of non-traumatized individuals on the human personality with the outcomes of those of people who are exposed to repeated psychological insults on a person during critical developmental periods (Herman, 1992).

Herman's developmental model follows closely along the lines of Donald Winnicott and the Object Relations theorists. For her, children develop in relationship to others with the interactions with primary caregivers serving as the template for all other relationships with the outside world to come (Herman, 1992). The primary caregivers are entrusted with the responsibility to provide for the child a sense of basic trust in the universe and in others. The child develops internalized representations of the stable and secure parents and the child is able to later turn to the "mental representations" in "times of stress" in order to find relief and a sense of competence (Herman, 1992).

This competence, over time begins to establish the person as capable of "initiative" and ultimately a sense of identity that allow the person to feel safe in relation to others (Herman, 1992). This identity, if securely established, allows the child to accomplish developmental milestones which further add to the child's sense of agency and personal power in the world. This sense of agency forms the basis for the development of a positive appraisal of the self.

Further, the relationship to the caregivers serve as a model of a "meaningful world" where others and their relationships with others are rewarding experiences that result in positive outcomes (Herman, 1992). Most of these developmental accomplishments are more felt than thought but the result is the same. A person who has come to view the world and his relationship to it as a positive (if challenging) experience for which he has the innate capacity to meet its demands. In this world, he loves and is loved.

His sense of self, based on the messages received from his caregivers, is strong and confident, loving and loved. Here, the child is now ready to face the world, to tackle more complex developmental challenges with the sense of initiative well established (Herman, 1992). But what of the child whose inner representations of others (and subsequently the self) is not stable? What if these representations are cold, controlling, cruel or inhumane? Here, Herman begins to make room in her formulation for the topic of this paper. Dissociation becomes a central feature of the traumatized individuals' personality organization and therefor sets him up to experience repeated trauma throughout his adult life.

For Herman, repeated exposure to trauma during early childhood "shatters the construction of the self that is formed in relation to others" (Herman, 1992, p. 51). The development of the sense of self is continually fractured by trauma to the point that the child does not develop a sense that the world is safe, that he is capable of meeting its demands or that others in that world are trustworthy. How then could one set out into the world with the necessary faculties in place when they have been exposed to trauma and had the development of their sense of self thwarted by destructive parenting? In Herman's world, the challenge is immense and potentially insurmountable.

Children exposed to trauma are unable to meet normal developmental tasks and are thus "prone to shame and doubt" (Herman, 1992, p. 52). For Herman, this doubt reflects one's inability to maintain a "separate point of view" while in relationship to to other people. Additionally, failure to achieve these milestones leave a person with feelings of shame and inferiority. Trauma thwarts competence. The individual in Herman's model who is filled with shame, inferiority and the inability to remain connected to his own vantage point in life when in relationship to others, is set up for future trauma. In fact, it is quite likely that trauma will follow him into him future.

The child who has been abused by those responsible for his care is unable to maintain a sense of relationship to community in the outside world (Herman, 1992). Their sense of trust in others and themselves is so frail that the person finds himself in perpetual ambivalence. On one hand, he has not established her sense of agency and power in the world so he is at its mercy, in desperate need of being taken care of. On the other hand, the people in it are untrustworthy, will victimize him or will at the very least become complicit in his abuse. A painful predicament if there ever was one.

So, what's a boy to do? According to Herman, much is done in service of trauma, and most of it is compensatory (Herman, 1992). Exposed to trauma and untrustworthy parents, the child develops defenses that are immature, not suited well for an autonomous life. A major defense employed by children (and later adults) who are exposed to trauma is dissociation. While many develop capacities that are both imaginative and creative, many are destructive "in which ordinary relations of body & mind, reality and imagination, knowledge and memory no longer hold" (Herman, p. 96).

The child here feels desperate. Unable to control his own body or thoughts due to the constant intrusion by caregivers, he is in constant scanning mode. Who he is becomes secondary to who he has to be to survive. Hyper-Vigilance develops here. In order to survive, the child must learn to anticipate danger at all costs (Herman, 1992). Over time, this hyper scanning feature becomes second nature, below conscious attention and therefore dissociated. The child becomes so attuned to potential danger, all other functions (like needs for satisfaction) become secondary. The child is a slave to his fear, just as he has been a slave to his parent's "totalitarian control" (Herman, p. 98).

Living in a world of a fear of "omnipresent death" (Herman, 1992, p. 98) leaves the child with pathological attachments to their caregivers. They still need them. After all, if you have no sense of confidence in your competence to accomplish life's tasks and the world is a frightening place, you need someone to take care of you. This predicament leaves the child isolated, keeping enough distance from the dangerous parent while remaining attached at all costs in order to survive. The helplessness experienced by the child in this environment is immense, he has no power and no ability to protect himself and in response, he first becomes hypervigilant and then learns to dissociate.

According to Herman, the abused child becomes "finely attuned to abusers inner states" and subtle changes in body language or facial movement become signals that danger is just around the corner (Herman, 1992). The child here has no time for developmental tasks, he is constantly on the lookout, afraid for his life. In many ways, this child is not present at all. I am reminded of Sullivan's "not me" self state. The child is so focused externally and on the internal states of others that he barely exists. Occurring outside of consciousness, the child becomes able to react to danger without really knowing it. He can spring into action without knowing why or what provoked it. These experiences are completely dissociated.

In this world, the child is faced with an enormous task: to find a way to attach to his caretakers who are negligent and dangerous; he must "trust the untrustworthy" (Herman, 1992, p. 101). At all costs, and with all of his "psychological adaptations" working in unison, his task is to maintain his primary attachment to the adults in his life (p. 101). In desperation, Herman describes the child as having two choices in front of him. He must rationalize the abuse so that those he needs are not completely dangerous or he must find a way to justify the abuse, to make himself at fault.

As part of the dissociative process, Herman states that these children often push the abuse out of their conscious awareness (Herman, 1992). The children here wish that they were not being abused and so they must keep it secret, even from themselves. Herman states that these children use "denial, voluntary suppression of thoughts and dissociative reactions and self induced trance" all in an attempt to keep the wish (and partial belief) that the abuse is not happening alive (p. 103).

Consciously however, the child is left with the consequences of the "bad me". Herman states that the development of a "bad me" explanation for abuse is in line with the childhood tendency to make oneself the reference point for everything that happens (Herman, 1992, p. 103). Parents add to the myth by "scapegoating" children and by blaming them overtly for the attacks that have just been leveled against them. This belief in the self as being bad is dissociated as well. While the child may be consciously aware of it initially as he rationalizes the terrifying abuse, over time, the belief becomes automatic, pre-conscious and cut off from conscious mind contents.

An additional consequence of the development of the "bad me" concept is that the child has internalized the evil of the abuser (Herman, 1992). This often results in compensatory behavior. The child may pretend to be a saint, attempting to placate others in fear of and in order to stave off an attack. According to Herman, these contradictory states cannot be integrated and so are dissociated. One cannot be both good or bad at the same time and so they become unconsciously separated from one another. One wonders if there is potential for narcissism to develop here. A compensatory development of an exaggeratedly good but false self that cannot be vulnerable.

Ultimately, Herman suggests that fragmentation of the personality is the consequence of these contradictory experiences of the self. "Fragmentation in consciousness prevents the ordinary integration of knowledge, memory, emotional states and bodily experiences". (Herman, 1992. p. 107) This fragmentation ultimately results in an inability to integrate the sense of self which prevents an integration of identity. Also, the fragmentation of others prevents the development of a sense of both independence and connection. This brilliant description of three very damaging consequences of the use of dissociation as a prophylactic defense are directly in line with the major question of this paper. If a person is fragmented in his sense of his own experience, his sense of self and his sense of others, is he not prone to be re-traumatized throughout her life?

Finally, Herman states that the traumatized child has three major forms of adaptation. There is an elaboration of dissociative defenses, a development of a fragmented identity and a pathological regulation of emotional states (Herman, 1992). Each of these is dissociative and each is ultimately maladaptive in adult life. It is difficult to imagine one with these defenses being used as primary means of coping with affective overload as not experiencing anxiety as a consequence of his interactions with the outside world.

Peter Levine -- Relationship and the Compulsion to Heal Trauma

Within it

In his seminal work on trauma and the ability to heal it's after effects called Waking The Tiger: Haling Trauma, (Levine, 1997), Peter Levine looks to the world of nature to describe common human reactions to trauma. "Trauma is part of a natural physiological process that simply has not been allowed to be completed" (Levine, 1997, p. 155). Levine insists that animals have a natural ability to discharge the energy that is created during a traumatic event that serves to protect to protect the victim and potentially save its life.

In his model, traumatic events stimulate the nervous system to encourage the animal (in this case human) to choose to fight, flight or freeze (Levine, 1997). Once the animal has recovered from the event, he or she may be able to recover once the event is over if the freeze option is selected. For non-human animals, the animal recovers and is able to go on with life after a mad dash into the woods upon waking from the trance that is induced by the overwhelmed-but-still working nervous system during the event. For the traumatized person however, the energy that was created and lead to the trance state due to a flooded mammalian brain, remains stored in the person and sets the stage for re-enactment.

For Levine, the compulsion to re-enact trauma lies in the same mechanisms that encourages rough and escape-oriented play in animals. Citing a television nature program, Levine insists that lion cubs who just experienced a trauma (an attack from an intruder)were re-enacting the event in the moments afterward, practicing new escape moves to be used in a potentially dangerous situation later (Levine, 1997).

For humans, the problem is in our advanced intelligence. Our evolved neocortex is at the heart of our difficulty recovering from trauma the way that animals do. The highly evolved neocortex becomes involved in re-enacting the event in order to search out potentially empowering future scenarios but is paralyzed by fear and terror which prevents it from working out a solution, thus leading the person to find themselves trapped in a "vicious cycle of fear and immobility, preventing the response from completing naturally" (p. 101).

The result? Hyper-vigilance. Levine's "undischarged arousal" leads the human neocortex to be bound in a cycle of perceived anxiety provoking situations that, over time, become intrinsically linked to the initial trauma (Levine, 1997). In fact, the fear becomes linked with any arousal and becomes nearly synonymous with the "vital energy" of survival itself (p. 151). Here, we can imagine Levine's victim of repeated trauma being unable to accept any new information as he is trapped by his hyper-vigilance and fear of new trauma. Might this play a role in preventing traumatized individuals from forming new relationships that do not end in repeating the trauma? If one is unable to take in information that is not "generalized" to all previous arousals linked to traumatic events, how is one to recognize a novel way of relating?

Levine's observations of traumatized individuals may offer some insight into the role that dissociation plays in keeping one in a cycle of trauma. If indeed, one does generalize all provocative stimuli occurring in relationships to the original traumatizing relationship, it is quite likely that one is both unaware of the extent that he is dissociated from his anxiety that is being provoked and unaware of how often he is presented with stimuli that is actually benign once he has been provoked.

While hyper-vigilance may activate a wild animal or even a person to potentially threatening environments and "others" in his range, it does not, however, extend his range of vision to include novel stimuli that are not threatening. All of us can attest to the impact of a bump in the night once we have been alerted to some other threatening sound. Our first thought is not that rusty old water heater in the basement.

If a process similar to stimulus generalization has taken place through repeated exposure to trauma then we can safely assume that the frequent occurrence of hypervigilant self states in the traumatized individual places them at a disadvantage in interpersonal relations with others. As he attempts to re-enact the events with an unconscious hope of recovery, he is drawn back into the trauma over and over again as his nervous system is activated by seemingly benign or even advantageous stimuli (i.e., sexual advances resulting in panic).

In this scenario, dissociation, plays the role of silent instigator as he is both dissociated from the relationship of the current stimuli to the one that resulted in trauma and dissociated from the potential of novel stimuli to result in a new event. An unconscious dilema ensues. Should I remain calm and open up to this new stimuli when it is so closely associated with so much pain in my past? Unfortunately, this question is never asked as all of these process are all unconscious (mammalian brain in origin or not).

Jessica Benjamin and a Developmental Model of Intersubjectivity

This paper accepts that a core concept of an inter-subjective model of personality development is an essential part of making a case for a constructivist approach to the unconscious. If we accept that the unconscious is not a static entity but an ever shifting

reference point from which any one individual in question operates,

we are then able to consider the possibility that repression is no

longer simply a matter of forgetting (actively or passively). From

here, we can begin to examine the possibility that the currents

shifting below the surface of one's outer presentation are waves of

unconscious motivation being created and destroyed in a moment by

moment, ever roiling sea of reactions.

Jessica Benjamin, using a developmental milestone model of

intersubjectivity (Mitchell, Aaron, 1999 p. 182) brilliantly

reconsiders the interpersonal model of personality in favor of one

that is truly inter-subjective (Benjamin, 1999 in Mitchell and Aron,

1999, p. 202). In her work *Recognition and Destruction: An Outline

of Intersubjectivity*, (1990) Benjamin posits that the ability to

recognize the subjective experience of the other is distinct from an

interpersonal model as proposed in the 1920s by Harry Stack

Sullivan (1937).

In her understanding of both the Object Relations theories of Winnicott and Interpersonal theories of Sullivan, the emphasis of emotional development through a separation-individuation process is heavily based on the infant's response to her reactions to the mother as an object, used in service of the infant (Benjamin, 1990, p. 186). Critiquing this viewpoint, Benjamin insists that the infant derives explicit joy from being in relationship not with a simple object from whom she can illicit any reaction she desires but from a subject who's responses are "not entirely predictable and assimilable" (Benjamin, 1990).

Benjamin also assails Heinz Kohut (largely credited as the father of Self Psychology) as missing the point. Pointing to Kohut's language that "self-objects" serve the function of "shoring up the self", Benjamin asks us to consider an extremely valid question (Benjamin, 1999). "At what point does it become the responsiveness of the outside other whom we love" (p. 187). Here, we are asked to move beyond the concept of internalized objects and into a world where one is not simply in relationship with an internal representation of a predictable object but in direct contact with a living, breathing, desiring and reacting other.

On the surface, it is possible to point to the work of Fairbairn who suggested that the infant does not "introject" objects that are not a source of anxiety (Guntrip, 1971) and is thus free to interact with anyone as a true other. Benjamin though, suggests something more. Rather than place the blame on an object who provokes anxiety in the infant who is unable to defend or provide for herself, she suggests that the conflicts that result in the inability to deal with the "other" as a recognizable other are intrinsic to the human psyche (Benjamin, 1990, p. 202). In fact, she suggests that the ability to recognize the other is a developmental milestone, only achievable when one is able to comes to terms with a workable dialectic between opposing tensions: one that is defined by a sense of omnipotence and the other by a "wish for contact" (Benjamin, 1990 p. 202).

Benjamin postulates that an infant, who has little tolerance for opposing sensations resorts to splitting (Benjamin, 1990).

Borrowing from Ogden, Benjamin (p. 204) suggests that over time however, a goal is that the chid (and future adult) begins to learn to cope with the natural tension between these two poles by allowing for a "recognizing third" (Ogden, 1994; Benjamin 1990), that allows one to recognize the subjective experience of the other without being overwhelmed by feelings that she will be lost if she allows herself to be impacted by the other in the dyadic relationship.

For Benjamin, the inter-subjective viewpoint is "guided by a palpable distinction between submitting to another's viewpoint and subordinating ourselves to certain kinds of necessity" (Benjamin, 1990 p. 207). Here the "struggle" between omnipotence and the need to connect is overcome by a sense of "working together to transcend complementarity in favor of mutual recognition (p. 208). In her remarkable commentary, Benjamin is moving beyond a simple argument over terminology regarding how we refer to the others we encounter but she is suggesting that in order to achieve true maturity in relation to the outside world, we must first learn to recognize (and even enjoy) the subjective experience of the other. Using the analytic relationship as a model, Benjamin makes the case for a truly inter-subjective theory based on the concept of recognition of the other.

As inspiring as Benjamin's suggestion that recognition and enjoyment of a true other within the mutually created frame of a "recognizing third" is, it is in the failure of achievement of this developmental milestone that this paper finds room for commentary on the potential for dissociation to play a role in the maintenance of trauma as a going concern rather than as a simple artifact of a tumultuous past.

If this milestone is not met, what then happens to the individual who is unable to recognize the subjective experience of the other? Does he miss valuable information about the potential intentions of the other, substituting actual dialog about said intentions with unconscious assumptions? Might he press ever forward, attempting to connect with the "introjected object" with a desire to connect while, simultaneously being frightened by the potential destruction of his omnipotence?

Without recognition of the other, the traumatized (and dissociated) person is left to fend for herself. While he genuinely desires to connect, his ability to do so is thwarted. Here, he finds himself caught in a storm of conflict. If he surrenders to the other, what will happen to him? Will he be dragged out to see, never able to maintain a footing on the shifting sand beneath his feet? In this scenario, he appears to be left with two options: to merge, truly losing himself in the experience of the other or to resist, fighting breathlessly against an undertow over which he has no control.

It is not impossible to imagine here that one who is unable to meet another without being caught in the maelstrom being at a serious disadvantage in relationship. We find a self comprised of dissociated self states who are ever shifting in reaction to the other, blindly moving toward and away from her, frightened of being connected, terrified of being abandoned. If, he does not learn to recognize the other without losing himself, it is easy to imagine projective identification following close on the heals of her projections as the other in the dyad struggles to find a way to be in a relationship where there is no room for his subjective experience. The potential for trauma here seems overwhelming.

Constructivist vs. Static Visions of the Unconscious Mind

Hirsch and Making Room for Dissociation in an Inter-Subjective

Model

Freud's model of personality development was largely dependent on a drive-based model of instincts that were at odds with one's ability to live in a world of civilized people. With this in mind, the unconscious was made up of material that had been "repressed" by the individual in order to reduce the tension created by those desires (Freud, 1989). This model naturally lends itself to an understanding of the unconscious as a static entity that is created and set in stone to be later uncovered with the aid of a skilled analyst. One's past is merely a set of memories that, because of their inaccessibility to conscious process, leave a person conflicted because of drives they do not understand and prohibitions based on experiences they can hardly remember.

In his paper *Changing Conceptions of Unconscious*, (1995) Irwin Hirsch examines the shift in understanding of personality development as being the consequences of undesirable drives and instincts poking through into daily activity and consciousness. Through self psychology-based developmental arrest models and into modern models that suggest that in order to truly understand the development of personality, one must comprehend a model that is innately and entirely inter-subjective.

Hirsch's understanding of the classical model can be summed up in a quote from the article: "The traditional view is an archeological method of detection, whereby hidden selves, fantasies, conflicts, or memories are uncovered in the form of historical truths, while the more recent, constructivist view holds that unconscious truth is relative and is discovered in the form of narrative truth" (Hirsch, 1995, p. 263). Here, Hirsch suggests that the unconscious is no longer a vertical column of historical facts but a horizontal field of beliefs, templates and object relations that is "relative" to experience, both past and present. The unconscious is no longer simply discovered, it is created over and over again using past experience as a guide and potentially as a predictor of future events.

Further, Hirsch points to the self psychology model of the unconscious as being a step in the right direction toward an inter-subjective model but eludes to its flaws in practice. Referring to the model as an "object relations" model, Hirsch suggests that while the emphasis on relationships with others or perceived others as the underlying, organizing principle of personality development, he also suggests that too much emphasis lies in a static understanding of the meaning of the unconscious and a view of analysis that consists of the analyst as an observer sitting on the outside of the therapeutic frame, an expert on human relationships. "As in the classical model, transference exists solely in the patient. The analysis can somehow transcend his or her subjectivity to observe or facilitate the unconscious. What may be lost in both models is the analyst's own idiosyncratic participation and the transference-countertransference matrix in which the analyst fully and unwittingly participates" (Hirsch, 1995, p. 266).

This "matrix" as Hirsch describes it is, as she also states, an extension of the work of Harry Stack Sullivan (Hirsch, 1995 p. 267). Citing Sullivan as "setting the stage for conceptualizing the unconscious, not as a singular, objective entity residing inside the patient, but rather as an experience reflecting the patient's interpersonal history that can be glimpsed through the analysts' subjective lens and participation" (p.267). Still, suggesting that his work does not go far enough, he rejects the notion that the analyst is outside of the dyad as an observer and states that he avoided "the examination of here-and now elements in the transference-countertransference matrix and placing the analyst as an observer of the patient's extra-transferential relationships" (p. 267).

For Hirsch, by removing the analyst from the dyad, much is missing in terms of helping the patient construct a narrative of his patterns of interpersonal relationships and it imagines that the unconscious is something made up of past templates of relating as opposed to being continually recreated in the "here and now" of the patient-analyst relationship.

Still, Hirsch looks to Sullivan and his accounts of anxiety (or anxiety avoidance) as being the thread that holds the fabric of (internal relational configurations" (Mitchell, 1988) together. In Hirsch's understanding of Sullivan, children "develop themselves around aspects of themselves that have been met with approval and may dissociate those aspects that have been met with disapproval" (Hirsch, 1995, p. 268). Here, we see the beginnings of the development of a definition of dissociation in his model that is based not on repressed memories from undesirable drives but as a consequence of relating to those who were formative in the young child's eyes.

Accepting the idea that anxiety and anxiety avoidance are at the core of the development of a "self-system" and it's role in the maintenance of relational patterns, Hirsch suggests that dissociation is a consequence of the person not paying attention to stimuli that would provoke anxiety or new information that could result in an unpredictable (and thus anxiety provoking) outcome. "Inattention, then is motivated by interpersonal anxiety and leads to both repression and lack of recognition" (Stern, 1983), which produces significant anxiety and may consequently lead to the development of a brittle sense of self (Hirsch, 1995, p. 268). Here, a picture emerges that depicts a young child as turning to his relational field for who and how to be in order to maintain his attachment to his those whose affection, nurturance and nutrition he is dependent upon.

Also accounting for the maintenance of this process throughout the lifespan, Hirsch points to the "rigidity" in which people hold onto these patterns that "truncate a more dimensional experience of living" due to an "adhesion to loved ones from the past with whom they are embedded and from whom they cannot separate" (Hirsch, 1992, p. 263); (Fairbairn, 1952; Feiner and Levinson, 1968-1969, Fromm, 1964; Schachtel, 1959; Searles, 1979). The suggestion being, if one's entire sense of self is dependent on a relational framework and that relational framework was based on traumatic abuse, rejection, inattention or a narcissistic extension of the caregiver's needs, then how is the now-adult infant to let go of those patterns without letting go of the self?

This process of self development comes at great cost however, as the person matures and is now expected to function in the outside world. This active self system may become so good at dissociation (conscious or unconscious), that new information about the potential of new experiences or even entire relationships is missed. "Dissociation narrows the range of potential experience and may lead to the inability to symbolize new incoming information" (Stern, 1983); (Hirsch, 1995). "By keeping things unformulated, the person can protect both himself and loved ones from anxiety. Unfortunately, this dynamic comes at considerable cost, since anxiety also interferes with the acquisition of new knowledge and the ability to think imaginatively" (Thompson. 1950); (Hirsch, 1995).

From this vantage point, we can see how dissociation as a result of the potentially-pathologically over-learned and desperately needed patterns of interpersonal relating could cultivate a cycle of re-traumatization that makes the possibility of escape by the suffering person extremely elusive. If, in the service of his need to control anxiety, a person continues to repeat a pattern of relating that was abusive and failed to meet his needs for affection and nurturance, how can he escape his identifications (Fairbairn, 1952) of his early life relationships with siblings, parents and others who were the source of the very template of what to expect from a life of relating to other people? This "quest for familial love and safety and the fear of disruption of self motivate this desire to stay in place, and fuel the repetition compulsion" (Russel, 1991 in (Hirsch. 1997, p. 269).

Finally, a point not explicitly made in Hirsch's article but that is inevitably left in the mind of the reader comes in the form of a question: to what extent will a person with an early history of traumatic abuse or rejection go to maintain the integrity of those ties? Will he not be able to stop until every new relationship satisfies his need to feel a certain kind of feeling that while temporarily satisfying may in fact provoke anxiety in the long term, feels familiar and somewhat safe? Hirsch briefly points to "anticipating or provoking abuse" and suggests that the more tenuous the ties to the caregiver the more tightly the person will cling to them as potential

extremes that one might go to in order to maintain ties (Hirsch, 1996,

p. 270) But this too begs additional questions.

When one is "anticipating or provoking abuse" might he be

actually turning his projections into projective identifications? If the

interpersonal field is a mutually influencing phenomenon (and I

believe it is), then will not (through behavioral and interpsychic

processes) the traumatized individual shape the behavior and

attitudes of the newly found loved ones until it resembles the much

loved abuser? Might the new lover herself switch from merely a

perceived potential abuser and her too become an abuser herself in

order to gain any recognition at all from her traumatized lover? Here

too, we see the role that dissociation might play in the dynamic

interplay of consciousnesses that are part of the inter-subjective

field.

Donnel B. Stern and Unformulated Experience

If we continue to think about a theory of personality (and an

unconscious) as a constructivist venture that is no longer one that is based on a warehouse of stored memories "stacked neatly like packing crates" (Stern, 1983, p. 77), we begin to understand the the concept of repression need no longer to be a consequence of "forgetting" whether purposefully or not. We can now imagine that what lies below the surface of consciousness outside of awareness may be things never fully learned in the first place. One need not forget something that was not attended to, formulated and symbolized in conscious thought.

In his groundbreaking paper on the concept of "unformulated experience" as a potential theoretical understanding of repression or the less commonly understood dissociation, Donnell B. Stern turns to the writing of Harry Stack Sullivan and even cognitive science. Stern postulates that dissociation is not simply a matter of repressing anxious thoughts but that there are a series of multilayered processes involved that are quite normal and natural to the human condition that at one time were a hallmark of developmental achievement but by now are are in service to a more insidious process that has an unwitting effect of contributing to the repeated folly of those who experienced a less than "good enough" caregiving environment (Stern, 1983).

According to Stern, cognition is not a given, rather it is continually created and recreated over time, "it is made" (Stern, 1983, p.72). This model differs greatly from one (like Freud's) where thoughts, perceptions and assumptions are automatic. There, one is obligated to assume that everything that is experienced is recorded, like a "film or tape library" (p.78). The emphasis here is on attention to experience and then a processing of that sensation into perception and ultimately symbolized into meaning.

For Stern, many areas of our existence are never formulated. While they may be witnessed by our eyes, felt on our skin or heard with our ears, we often are so quickly shifted from event to event that attention is not paid to them and the experience is lost to time in a vague drift of experience. Going further, Stern suggests that we depend on this selective attention process for survival in order to make the world make sense and contain symbolic meaning (Stern, 1983).

"Unformulated material is experience which has never been fully articulated clearly enough to allow application of the traditional defensive operations" (Stern, 1983, p. 73). Here, Stern contrasts unformulated experience from traditional defensive operations which rely on a purposeful (or instinctive) forgetting of experience. What Stern suggests is that these experiences were never formulated at all, leaving room for new interpretations of the particular mechanisms that might be involved in dissociation.

"Defensively motivated unformulated experience is a kind of 'familiar chaos' to borrow a phrase from Paul Valery, a state of mind cultivated and perpetuated in the service of the wish to not think" (Stern, 1983, p. 72). This "wish to not think" is at the heart of the matter of dissociation. Speaking of the familiarity that is maintained by "defensive unformulated experience", Stern goes on: "Familiarity is it's camouflage. Defensively motivated unformulated experience is a lack of clarity and differentiation permitted or encouraged in cognitive material that, in a more completed form, would be noxious" (p. 72).

For an explanation of how this habit of "motivated unformulated experience" can turn on a person as life progresses, Stern turns once again to Sullivan's self-system. "The self-system includes all those experiences and ways of relating to others which have been found through experience to be safe and secure. Or from the other direction: The self-system rejects all experiences and modes of relating which are associated with anxiety " (Stern, 1983, p. 73). In other words, the self-system is an unconscious means of regulating anxiety by protecting the person's overall perception of himself.

Unfortunately, in order to maintain this sense of self and avoid anxiety, the self-system naturally leaves out other information. Like the infant who learns to recognize the voices of those who are safety and security providing figures and screens out those who provoke anxiety, a self system that has been organized around intense anxiety and fear can no longer recognize new information as it is constantly screening out this "general cognitive function". That which once served the infant well in order to facilitate bonding now leaves him with an inability to seek out novel stimuli in relationship

as those stimuli were long learned to be avoided due to the anxiety

they provoked (Stern, 1983, p. 74).

Further citing Sullivan to support his theory that infants (and

adults) are unintentionally screening their experience to avoid

potential anxiety, Stern cites three ways of understanding employed

by infants attempting to comprehend their world. Prototaxic

experiences are those that merely drift by the infant with little or no

relationship to those that came before or afterward (Stern, 1983).

Parataxic experiences are those that are now broken up into

manageable pieces but are not related to one another in organized

ways.

Finally, syntaxic experiences are those that have been

attended to, reflected on and now have meaning to one another

through the symbolic processes of organized thought and ultimately

language. Presented sequentially like developmental milestones,

Stern (and Sullivan from his point of view) makes the case that learning to organize experience using thought and language is a hallmark of maturation.

Unformulated experience as a consequence of dissociation is material never attended to. "It remains organized at the parataxic level" he states (Stern, 1983, p. 75). While this material may have had it's potential to provoke anxiety thwarted since it has never been reflected upon it has also not been learned and thus reflected upon.

And so, it is easy to imagine that without attention paid to experiences that are avoided based on their potential to provoke anxiety, the thoughts are never had and understanding of their meaning is never reached. Like the woods depicted at the edge of town in the M. Night Shyamalan thriller "*The Village*", what is most frightening (and most anxiety provoking in the long term) is exactly what resides beneath the canopy of trees (Shyamalan, 2004). That cannot be known as long as one stays as far away from the woods as she can get.

Stern cites Sullivan as suggesting that dissociated material makes people anxious because they have never thought about it. The self system is "built around these gaps in experience" and thus the "dissociation must be perpetuated" (Stern, 1983, p. 76). So, while the person may not ever get any closer to knowing what is at the heart of the unknown fear they experience, they do get the benefit of putting two and two together and experiencing what was unthinkable to experience before. As Stern puts it, the dissociated space is "an element of the self so vital to it's integrity as, say, the white space is to the visual structure of a painting" (p. 76).

The self-system will protect itself. It may prevent one from experiencing an anxiety that was re-experienced as part of early life so often that it is now essential to the survival of self that in order to access (and reconstruct) that dissociated material, the person is potentially threatened at the very core of her existence. Just as filling the white space of a work of art threatens the integrity of a masterpiece, so too does pursuing lines of thought and symbolic construction that were previously prohibited threaten the structural integrity of the self. The clinical implications are clear.

In order to provide support for the constructivist theory of unformulated experience and thus dissociation, Stern turns to the world of cognitive science for answers. Citing the "information processing" model of cognition, Stern suggests that "mental activity is seen as organic, continuous, and unitary. New experiences are not simply added on like the crates stacked in a warehouse, but integrated with everything that has come before (Stern, 1983, p. 79).

Adding that Piaget suggested that new information is both assimilated into the old understanding of things and that the new information actually can change the old schemata of organization as well. Dovetailing nicely, Stern points to research that suggests that memory is a function of multiple process that begins the "moment the stimulus hits the sense receptor, through perception, into consciousness and short-term memory, and eventually into long-term memory, where the information is used for a variety of purposes" (Stern, 1983, p. 79). During each of the above mentioned phases, the information is changed, becoming more "clearly articulated". (p.80).

Here, we can imagine that events that are experienced can not only be forgotten or distorted, they may never make it into memory. Over time, if these events are never converted to long-term memory, they are left unformulated. Citing Neisser, a founder of cognitive psychology, Stern describes the processes that occur most proximally to experience and demonstrates how they are altered and changed both by the information that came before it and information that comes after. Adding further evidence to the idea that experience (and the memory and meaning of that experience) are created (Stern, 1983).

Stern cites two stages based on Neisser's work. The first is an ionic stage where information is first experienced and is organized in large pieces by the experiencer. In this phase, information is kept in a short-term storage container for use in further processing. Items in this container that do not receive attention, are forgotten or better yet, never learned, left unformatted (Stern, 1983).

In the second phase, information that is attended to is reified and committed to memory, not as a static memory but as a constructed memory that is able to be altered in the future when new information is provided (Stern, 1983). Thus, while we may remember an event based on certain details that were salient to us for a variety of reasons at the time of the event and shortly thereafter, we may forget what we were wearing that day or even figures in the event who were not particularly of interest.

Moving the process into a mental activity rather than just a external event, Stern suggests that our ruminations, partial thoughts, memories and even vague perceptions are constantly triggered both by external and internal experience and are selectively attended to with only partial understanding of the contents. The rest remains unformulated and left in the "familiar chaos" that contained it before (Stern, 1983, p. 82).

It is this "selective attention" process that is largely unconscious so long as we leave it in place. This is the self-system operating smoothly, just as Sullivan had envisioned it. Stern suggests that there is reason to believe that one (among many) factors that may be at work at speeds so fast that we are normally not aware of them is the reduction or avoidance of anxiety (Stern, 1983). I would add, not simply the anxiety provoked by the partial memory or "unformulated experience" itself but by an underlying anxiety of vague threats to the structure of the perception of self.

In a further explanation of the process of selective attention, Stern suggests that long term memory can also feed back on one's ability to process new information. "Long term memory can feed back to the very beginning of the process of thought, extrapolate the eventual form the unformulated material would take if it entered consciousness, and on that basis select what material will be processed further and what material will be allowed to decay (Broadbent, 1958; Deutsch and Deutsch, 1963; Stern, 1983).

Forming what Neisser called an "executive" function that is telling lower functions how to operate. This executive (unconscious or at least faster than thought) has the ultimate say on what gets formulated and thus remembered (Neisser, 1967 in Stern, 1983). Further, Stern suggests that the executive can also "terminate processing on the basis of disturbing glimmers of meaning of which we are aware, at least for moments" (p. 84). These cognitive processes shed light on phenomenological experiences that we all know to be anecdotally true. We have all had dinner with the bickering couple who, while telling a simple story get sidetracked into detail on what color the outfit she was wearing, each swearing to the "god's honest truth". While one may never know what color she was actually wearing, we know that they are both equally convinced of their experience for totally different reasons. It is also quite certain that neither ever consciously decided to take the other position just for the fun of it.

Stern's commentary on unformulated experience is extremely relevant to the exploration set upon in this paper. If analytic tradition can be informed by cognitive science than our understanding of what it means to dissociate is expanded. By allowing our understanding of personality to be constructivist in nature, we allow ourselves to accept that the self is not a fixed entity but one that is created over time and mutually recreated in relationship. Here, experience is not merely forgotten, it is yet to be fully experienced (Stern, 1983).

If one's self system is actively working on his behalf to avoid anxiety, we must accept that it is also avoiding some new information. This new information may be vital in helping someone learn a new relational style rather than continue to be avoided because the circumstances that created the tendency to relate this way were too painful to commit to memory. This experience, of course will never be formulated exactly as it occurred at that moment both because experience is always subjectively created and because there is no actually memory to begin with. What can be done however, is to learn to allow our attention to focus when we feel those glimmers of anxiety rising up and turn them into glimmers of hope. Hope for a better understanding of our process, hope for a new levels of tolerance for our own very subjective experience and hope for a new and different outcome in the future.

Dissociation is Experience not Coded Into Language:

Hirsch and a New Understanding of Dissociation Within a

Relational/Inter-subjective/Affect Regulation Matrix.

Adding to the discussion of the widening of the concept of the unconscious and as a consequence, the notion of dissociation is an article titled World Horizons: A Post-Cartesian Alternative to the Freudian Unconscious by Robert Stolorow, Donna Orange and George Atwood (2001). Shifting the emphasis of analysis from the "privileged knowledge of the unconscious" (p. 44), the team insists that we can no longer imagine the unconscious as a container maintained within the larger structure of the self for which the analyst holds the key. Instead, the unconscious should be pictured as "an experiential system of expectations, interpretive patterns, and meanings, especially those formatted in the context of psychological trauma, losses, deprivations, shocks, injuries, violations and the like" (p. 46.).

When thought about this way, we no longer are satisfied with a metaphor for human experience that is limited to a vertical organization of experience. Here, humans are free to organize their "emotional and relational experiences so as to exclude whatever feels unacceptable, intolerable, or too dangerous in particular inter-subjective contexts" (Stolorow et al., 2001, p. 46). The implications on the process of dissociation are considerable. Previously, repression was considered the primary mechanism by which static, fully formed memories are lost in locked "containers" waiting for the all-knowing but stoic analyst to come along and unlock the door with his wealth of knowledge.

Instead, dissociation becomes an active process always occurring, always influencing what has come before it, along with what is being dissociated. The general nature of this powerful defense changes as does our ability to do something about it. Analysis now becomes a dialog between two mutually influencing partners who, while sitting together create dialog that has the potential to spark new creative spaces where one is able to recognize where she has been dissociating and how those patterns of learning (or not learning) information have been preventing her expansion. "Psychoanalysis aims to expand the patient's horizons, thereby opening up the possibility of an enriched, more complex, and more flexible emotional life" (Stolorow, et al., 2001, p. 47.) Analysis has now been moved from a study of the past to being an exploration of the present and the future, an optimistic premise indeed.

Contrasting with Freud's "repression barrier" Stolorow, et al., describes "emergent properties of an ongoing, dynamic, relational system" that is engaged in an ongoing pattern of relational dissociation. In this view, the concept of repression of undesirable drives and urges is shifted to the back burner in favor of a viewpoint that considers the relational experience of the person to the outside world, how that world is impacting her and what "she is capable of knowing" as a consequence of her style of learning and relating (Stolorow, et al., 2001, p. 48).

Stolorow, et al., explores two types of dissociation, the first concerning the emotional neglect of an infant. "When a child's experiences are consistently not responded to and are actively rejected, the child perceives that aspects of his or her own experience are unwelcome or damaging to the caregiver. These regions of a child's experiential world must then be sacrificed in order to safeguard the needed tie" (Stolorow, et al., 2001, p. 48). Here, the process of ego development is taken into account and the environment is considered to play a significant role. The child in this scenario, just as she is awakening to a sense of self, beings to know what will keep her close and what will separate from her needed caregiver. In the infant whose very survival depends upon the love and nourishment of the caregiver, there is no choice.

This process whereby the infant "unconsciously" learns to respond to the caregiver's needs leaves many areas of the child's experiential world "unvalidated" (Stolorow, et al., 2001, p. 48.). Eventually as those areas of consciousness begin to fade into the past due to a lack of recognition, reward or validation, it is as if they have never happened at all. In fact, eventually they will not. This is the essence of "unformulated experience". The infant "learns" though the process happens so fast that its occurrence could easily be called unconscious to avoid certain behaviors, emotional spaces or even cognitions themselves. The material has never been "brought into consciousness" (Stolorow, et al., 2001, p. 48). As the authors describe it, there is a total "absence of a validating inter-subjective context" (Stolorow, et al., 2001, p. 49). This might be thought of ike a conversation that never happened.

Pointing to the pre-verbal period in a child's life, while she is learning to symbolize her world eventually into the area of language, the process is shaping the symbolizing style and capacity of the infant. The child, through "attunement" with the caregiver in a "sensorimotor dialog" learns what can and cannot be symbolized without consequence. As more and more of her consciousness becomes symbolized, what is left unconscious remains unsymbolized. This "refusal to interpret" (Stern, 1997), is at the heart of dissociation from this point of view.

Using case material to illustrate the importance of affect regulation to the concept of dissociation, the authors point to a reformulation of a case from an inter-subjective perspective. Stern, demonstrating an infant's desire to regulate her affect in order to appease the caregiver, we are told of a young woman who, in a troubled relationship with her mother, has managed to keep out of awareness deep feelings of "aloneness and vulnerability" that very likely were picked up in the earliest days of life when her traumatized mother who herself lost her husband to the Nazis was unable to tolerate her young daughter's affective reaction to her father's death (Stolorow, et al., 2001).

To imagine dissociation as a consequence of affect regulation is to consider the importance of relationship in the development of personality. We learn to regulate affect at the earliest age and we do so in relationship to significant others. As this relational style takes hold, we become captive to it, never knowing what we do not know. So good at managing anxiety (or potential anxiety) is this affective regulation system that we are often left flying blind, without instruments, at the mercy of the fog. Perpetually, we recreate our own fog without knowing it by turning away from that which scares us and reminds us of the unspeakable terror that we know is out there, the terror of the loss of those who are entrusted with our care.

Hirsch: The Widening Concept of Dissociation

In the conversation over repression vs. dissociation, it is worth noting that at one time, repression was considered to be the "more common and normal way that experience was rendered out of consciousness" (Hirsch, 1997, p. 603). Events were thought to have been fully processed and then forgotten, like a dusty cardboard box in the attic of our unconscious. And as such, it was thought that analyzability was directly related to how much material was repressed and not dissociated.

Irwin Hirsch, echoing the sentiments of Donnell Stern asks us to consider that dissociation is far more common and recurrent than repression (Hirsch, 1997). From the banal to the traumatic, various systems (what Sullivan might call self systems) are at work to maintain our sense of self and a coherent perceptual frame in order to avoid psychic overload. From the color of the sky to the look in an intimate's eye. we have reason to block from consciousness perspectives that we do not wish to participate in. At times non-defensive and at other times, rallying all of our defenses at once, dissociation is both an every day psychic phenomenon and a reaction to frightening (or potentially frightening) stimuli.

"The same psychic operations that lead to severe restrictions and psychopathology, under kinder conditions, lead to normal and neurotic problems in living (Hirsch, 1997, p. 606). According to Hirsch, "it's all a matter of degree". Shifting defense from pure pathology to normal operations that are profoundly subverted is essentially in line with a modern approach to psychopathology. In a relational matrix, it is the particular response to the inter-subjective field that matters much more than mechanisms that are pathological in and of themselves.

Pursuing a discussion of the process of identification, Hirsch asks us to consider the subtleties of "intimate engagement that forms the stuff of internalized self-other configurations in the first place" (Hirsch, 1997, p. 605). In this model, Hirsch suggests that each and every significant relating experience we have contributes to the template we carry around with us; what she refers to as "identifications" (p. 605).

While we do not know that we are identifying while we are doing so, we are still repeating that process. That person who reminds us of someone that we cannot remember is perhaps an everyday example of this phenomenon at work. If those early relational experiences are "based in conflict" then it becomes increasingly likely that our identifications, (i.e., those we recognize) are also likely to include conflict and all of the surrounding potential for trauma that accompanies them Hirsch, 1997, p. 605). All of this process occurs, of course, without our explicit awareness and therefore is dissociative.

Hirsch like Stern asks us to consider the possibility that dissociation is not merely a pathological phenomena but an organic function of the self organizing operations of the average human being. All of us must learn to define our experience by expectations in order to avoid "psychic overload" of all kinds, even if it is banal. When considered from this perspective, dissociation is more comprehensible to us, and more human. Just as we consciously sort through a restaurant menu to determine what will bring us pleasure as we consume it, so do we unconsciously sort through experience in order to maintain our sense of ourselves and our place in the world.

Quantitative Evidence for Dissociation as a Major Feature of Repeated Trauma

As has been mentioned before in this paper, a significant feature of people who are diagnosed with personality disorders is the use of dissociation as a primary defense. The inability to recognize their own shifts in self state or the subjective experience of another can have major implications on someone's relational style. Additionally, as clinicians, we recognize a unique type of "pull" to respond to particular individuals as oftentimes the transferential field becomes oppressive or at least unrecognized in any verbalized or otherwise noticeable way by our current patient.

Very often, patients who exhibit these symptoms are diagnosed in "Cluster B" of the Diagnostic and Statistical Manual of Mental Disorders IV TR (DSM IV TR, 2000) in general and Borderline Personality Disorder in particular. When working with people with this diagnosis, we become acutely aware of the challenges faced by them when so much of their experience is "syntonic" that is, contained only within a vision of their experience that remains unchallenged. And, we understand how difficult life must be when many of the nonverbal and verbal cues that usually exist in the interpersonal field are invisible. The relational challenges for "borderlines" are immense.

Further, when we think about Borderline Personality Disorder, we think of trauma. Research has frequently demonstrated that there is a high correlation of the experience of repeated trauma and the diagnosis of BPD (Putnam, 1989). We also know that from clinical experience. As has been frequently suggested in this paper, early childhood trauma (particularly when perpetrated by a close caregiver who is essential to the child's well being) has a profoundly deleterious influence on the eventual relational style of these people when they become adults. When they tell their stories, we are often shocked and saddened by the burdens that were experienced at such young ages by such fragile egos. The damage to the developing sense of self can be devastating.

Seeking to establish a link between survivors of childhood trauma with BPD and the defense of dissociation, researchers in

Australia performed a quantitative analysis of a study performed with Borderlines measuring their tendency to use dissociation as a defense mechanism (Watson, Chilton, and Peter, 2006). While their findings may not be startling to those of who have treated people with Borderline Personality Disorder in a clinical setting, they are nonetheless helpful in that they establish quantitative evidence to support what is well known clinically.

Using a study of 139 participants who had been diagnosed with Borderline Personality Disorder, the researchers determined that participants who endorsed more items confirming early childhood abuse on the "Childhood Trauma Questionnaire" also tended to endorse items indicating greater dissociative experiences on the "Dissociative Experience Scale" compared to those who had not endorsed similarly on the CTS (Watson, et al., 2006).

This study and others like it establish in a quantitative and empirical way much of what this paper hold as a major argument. That is that early childhood experiences that are traumatic and abusive can lead to challenges in relating to others, particularly in the area of the use of dissociation as a defense mechanism which is a hallmark of Borderline Personality Disorder.

Dissociation as a Major Feature Complex PTSD

Judith Herman, a leading thinker in the area of trauma coined the term "Complex PTSD" in her groundbreaking book Trauma and Recovery. (Herman, 1992). Herman set out to carve out a unique diagnosis for those whose exposure to trauma was experienced not as a single event but as recurrent experience. In her description, she refers to one who ultimately left the victim of such trauma powerless and, practically speaking, captive to a set of circumstances involving a perpetrator or perpetrators who repeatedly neglected, sexually abused or otherwise brutalized a person until their very sense of self became disturbed. She called her diagnosis "Complex PTSD", (Herman, 1992). That experience (and the groundbreaking work that depicts it) is well documented in another area of this paper.

In an effort to establish a link between Complex PTSD and dissociation, a team of researchers spanning from the Utrecht University in The Netherlands to a clinical psychologist in Atlanta Georgia looked to identify patterns (Van der Hart, O., Nijenhuis, R., and Steele, K., 2005). In a bold claim, the researchers suggest that dissociation is not merely a symptom of Complex PTSD but that it is a "common psychobiological pathology", dividing the personality into "biphasic patterns as a manifestation of trauma-related structural dissociation or division of the personality" (Van der Hart, et al., 2005, p. 2).

The article appearing in the Journal of Traumatic Stress (Van der Hart, et al., 2005), looked at victims of "threatening caregivers" and found that dissociation of personality develops when children or adults are exposed to potentially traumatizing events when their integrative capacity is insufficient to (fully) integrate these experiences within the confines of a relatively coherent personality. The authors see the divisions between areas of the personality in much the same way that Sullivan might describe different self-states that lack access to one another.

The authors define personality as "action subsystems" that shape personality and that each of these subsystems is defined by qualitatively different perceptual, sensory and cognitive processing that are accompanied even by physiological changes (Clynes and Panskepp, 1988, p. 48). And, within these subsystems are "situationally accessible memories (SAM)" that may not be not be accessed intentionally but are triggered by emotionally provocative stimuli (Van der Hart, et al., 2005, p. 10).

Within these subsystems also are differences in affects and impulses (Van der Hart, et al., 2005), alterations in self-perception, alterations in relations with others and alterations in systems of meaning. For the authors of this study, distinct personality styles are seen and these different styles are experienced as being perpetuated by completely different people (p. 8). The person experiencing this may or may not even be aware of this as happening. This "structural dissociation" involves "alternating dominance of and limited interactions between dissociated parts dedicated to daily life and avoidant of traumatic memories and parts dedicated to defense in response to threat and fixated in traumatic experience" (p. 11).

While it is not clear (and potentially never will be) whether or not there are structurally different parts of the personality in an empirically documentable way, the essential suggestion of this article remains profound if only because the experience is felt as structural by both the person and her relational other in a phenomenological way. Like other authors that this article has discussed in order to suggest that dissociation is a defensive method employed to keep disturbing or otherwise unwelcome out of consciousness, the authors here have described a unique perspective on the potential experience of dissociation.

If the authors are correct and there indeed are unique affective, informational and even physiological characteristics to these individual subsystems than dissociated self states would indeed be a frightening thing to integrate. The author explicitly suggests that integration of these subsystems should be a goal of treatment when working with dissociative disorders. However if one version of the self has access to frightening experiences that another does not, there is likely a good reason for that. And from this point of view, it is easy to imagine this process as potentially adaptive. In a world where terror is so all encompassing that one must escape to a new reality in order to feel secure, one certainly cannot be blamed for doing so.

Trauma, Conflict and Re-Enactment:

Bromberg and Enactment as A Desire to Heal

Furthering the discussion of modern theoretical implications on dissociation is Philip Bromberg who borrows heavily from the work of Harry Stack Sullivan. Emphasizing the need to conceptualize reality as a construct that is made in relationship of self to other AND in relationship from self to self, rather than merely an objective reality that is witnessed, Bromberg describes a tension that exists within the individual as he attempts to recognize and be recognized while maintaining a coherent conceptualization of the self (Bromberg, 1993).

Of the the inherent difficulties he writes that there is "the interplay between an individual's capacity to access and cognitively process dissociated perceptual experience (past and present) and his felt vulnerability to potential traumatic disruption of his ongoing feeling of selfhood" (Bromberg, 1993 , p. 149). Using the analytic dyad as a primary metaphor for the enactment of this tension, Bromberg lays out a case for dissociation of self states as a result of traumatic shock and the fear of it as being central to the operational style of individuals who use dissociative mechanisms as their predominant operational style.

In an encouragingly optimistic view of enactment within the analytic dyad, Bromberg writes that patients present to treatment with an expectation of healing and that the process of enactment is a frustrated but hopeful attempt to be known and recognized in that knowing (Bromberg, 1993). For Bromberg, all patients' realities are in "a dialectic with perception and his unconscious fantasies of relationship but the analysand who is locked in a pattern of enactment of dissociated self states is unable to experience any objective experience of themselves and are hoping that if the analyst can perceive them that they too can".

The difficulties experienced by Bromberg's patients is at the heart of this paper. In his paper, he helps to illustrate the process that culminates in retraumatization while protecting the experience of the traumatized individual person. For Bromberg, enactment is an opportunity for the individual to express his unconscious wishes in the context of the relationship (Bromberg, 1993). In these dissociated states, the person lacks the recognition of the process that is occurring but in the analytic dyad, now has a new tool for finding a viewpoint from which he may see himself.

Seeing the self states of a client who's boundaries are porous, as a reflection of a "personality organization not yet sufficiently cohesive to hold simultaneously the need to make contact, the experience of having been given permission to do so, and the ability to empathize with the analyst's own legitimate limits", Bromberg asks us to consider that at this point of intrusion and potential rejection, a traumatized individual is attempting to make contact through this "relational act" and provides the potential for the "potential trauma to be cognitively processed" (Bromberg, 1993, p. 152).

In Bromberg's understanding, dissociation is an attempt to kill the trauma and it holds the potential to ward off new trauma. The dissociative personality is ever in fear of being retraumatized and dissociation of consciousness between self states allows those selves to be so separated from one another that the fear of shock cannot be experienced (Bromberg, 1993). The consequences for such use of the defense are enormous however as not only is painful contact with a frightened self-state denied, so is the ability to objectively experience the worlds that each inhabit, leaving the person with no constant perceptual framework with which he might organize his experience. No self.

This too is elaborated in Bromberg's piece. Stating succinctly that there is no real self but rather a collection of "subnarratives" that accompany various self states, Bromberg makes explicit his belief that the inability to experience (or even remember) one self-state while in another tremendously inhibits one's ability to experience himself as a real entity (Bromberg, 1993, p. 161). Acknowledging the inherent paradox of the intention of dissociation as a prophylactic for the self, Bromberg points to the growing conception that consciousness is not originated as a whole that disintegrates over time but one that begins with inchoate experiences and gathers and solidifies over time. From this point of view, it can be understood that the problem is not that the self has disintegrated, it is that as a consequence of shocking, early traumatic experience, the self never fully integrated in the first place.

Here we see the makings of a personality structure that is incapable of experiencing dissociated parts of itself and the repercussions of such organization. According to Bromberg, he is incapable of holding conflicting ways of seeing himself within a "single experiential state long enough to feel the subjective pull of opposing affects" (Bromberg, 1993, p. 163). The result is an inability to experience conflict, the hallmark of maturity in psychoanalytic terms. This subjective isolation of self-states from one another is at the very core of the problem of retraumatization. Without the helpful eye of an observing ego, one is essentially lost at sea. As wave after wave of self-states wash over him, he is unable to know what has just happened or even what will happen, he is perpetually in the moment with no option to reflect on what is happening to them.

Finally, Bromberg too points to cognitive science as evidence to support his theory. Stating that amnesia accompanies shifts between self-states, he calls attention to the research done by Bonanno in the area of memory that suggests that it is created as it is accessed and is by no means a static entity but rather exists as a perpetually reinterpreted comprehension of experience (Bromberg, 1993). In particular, memories around highly emotionally charged experiences tend to be most "deprived of a self content" as these memories are denied by unconscious processes associated with dissociation (p. 164).

In Bromberg's worldview, there is in innate collision between the desire to relate and the need to preserve a coherent sense of self (Bromberg, 1993). If this is true and this experience is universal among people who have not experienced repeated early life trauma, how then will those who have experience this collision? If this collision was experienced as terrifying or "shocking" to use Bromberg's language, how then will he be able to allow himself (let alone others) to experience his self in relationship. By dissociating the self-states that either experienced or continue to fear experiencing trauma, the self is protected in a moment to moment stand-off with fear. The trouble is, the battle is never over as he is unable to access those isolated parts of himself in dialog with one another and with an observing ego. And so, the cycle of trauma continues.

Bromberg and the role of Shame, An Inability to Tolerate Conflict
and the Always Anticipating Trauma System

Attempting to bring the defense of dissociation forward from simply being about keeping one from experiencing the painful and traumatic events of the past, Philip Bromberg in his essay Potholes on the Royal Road: Or is it an Abyss (Bromberg, 2000). asks us to consider the role of enactment, shock and shame in the dissociative process. Citing "shock" as the hallmark of trauma, Bromberg reminds us that shock and the desire to avoid repeating it are at the core of enactment which is how the therapeutic dyad experiences dissociation in the current moment.

As a person who has experienced repeated trauma goes through life, she is attempting to maintain ties with caregivers who were essential to her safety. In order to do so, she must keep those relationships alive and in the moment, she does so through enactment (Bromberg, 2000) Unfortunately, contained within that enactment is the potential for shock and as she enters those self-states where that shock is contained, she is likely to be triggered and unconsciously shift away from that self-state in order to avoid that shock. Here, Bromberg points directly at the area where dissociation is the most destructive.

As we move through life, attempting to heal our old wounds, we try as we might to relate to others as if they are new. Unfortunately, for those who have been repeatedly traumatized, the "unrelenting repetitiveness of certain enactments is more likely to eventuate his feeling closer and closer to an abyss" (Bromberg, 2000, p. 7). That abyss, is a fear of a loss of self as experienced during the traumatizing events. If the edge of an emotional cliff is looming on the horizon, dissociation is a logical way to avoid falling over. The trouble is, one is unable to learn if this time, one might not have gone over. Dissociation may serve one well but just as surely, it has the potential to be one's master.

Bromberg points to shame as another area where dissociation is a going concern rather than as a vault for the objets of the past

(Bromberg, 2000). In shame, a person is left feeling isolated and un-soothed in the face of re-experiencing trauma, just like she felt when she was experiencing the abuse or neglect that comprised her trauma. It is no wonder then that avoiding the experience of shame through dissociative processes would make sense. Shame is such a central part of the experience of helplessness experienced by so many trauma victims that is itself becomes something to fear and something to avoid.

The unconscious process of avoiding shame is also connected to Bromberg's theory that an inability to experience conflict is another component of dissociative processes. In his model, achievement of conflict is a developmental goal in successful analysis (Bromberg, 2000). Only by bringing these unconscious (dissociated) experiences into psychic tension is one able to utilize the processes of learning to metabolize them. Shame, being an example of an emotional state that no one wants to experience for fear that she will not be soothed, is a prime example of the kind of conflict that is not being experienced in dissociated states. The central conflict in shame is a lack of autonomy in the presence of others, an incredible sense of vulnerability.

The central theme of this paper is that trauma and the threat of retraumatization never really goes away for those who have lived it. By pointing to shame, enactment and the inability to experience interpsychic conflict, Bromberg asks us to consider the incredible feats of bravery we are asking our patients to undertake when we ask them to first explore and then to integrate their dissociated states. The potential for retraumatization, not necessarily by another rapist, abuser or neglectful parent but by the experience of shame and internal conflict is a frightening potentiality and understanding what is at stake for our clients by entering these domains helps us to better empathize with their experiences.

Stern and the Self States: Dissociation, Enactment and

Understanding

"Contexts... are enveloping atmospheres, at least as much as matters of mood or affect as of content, within which some kinds of experience and interaction can take shape and others cannot" (Stern, 2003, p. 843). Donnell Stern in his paper The Fusion of Horizons: Dissociation, Enactment and Understanding, (Stern, 2003) examines the areas of speech, context, self-states and enactment and describes the role that they play in contributing to dissociation, it's prophylactic effects and it's long term consequences in the life of one who uses dissociation a primary mode of operation and on it's impact in analysis.

By describing his clinical experience and his times of being able to join his clients within the context of their varied self-states, Stern moves the discussion of dissociation forward beyond a description of one particular defense and into a realm of true understanding of the phenomenological experiences held by the one who is dissociating. Describing this process, he states as "a fusion must first occur inside of the the analyst's experience, a fusion between the horizon of what-feels-like-me and the horizon of part-of-me that feels alien, the other inside of myself" (p. Stern, 2003, 844). Of course, he is talking about the analytic dyad in this quote but he is also describing what has been required of him in order to truly experience dissociation with his clients first hand.

Going on, Stern states that we are only able to truly understand the behavior of another when we understand the "self-state from which it arose" (Stern, 2003, p. 845). A herculean task if ever there were one, Stern is fleshing out his understanding of a process that is not easily described using traditional empirical research methods. It is only in the dyadic context of two people committed to their mutual desire to understand their impact on one another that one is really able to grasp in a truly intuitive way, what this process is all about. And here, Stern makes a major contribution to this work. A key element of the method of study in this work is the understanding that it is my goal to understand dissociative processes from the perspective of those who have experienced it and that is why this work relies so heavily on psychoanalytic literature. In many ways, it is the only research (aside from qualitative interviewing and possibly various art forms) that one is able to get a "rich description" from the inside of the process.

In noticing various disconnects in the analytic process, Stern states that often, these separations are "dynamically enforced separation, or dissociation, of the analysts relevant self states" (Stern, 2003, p. 845). Here, in a kind of analytic parallel process, Stern is able to experience dissociation first hand as it occurs in his inter-subjective field with the analysand. Going further, Stern considers the possibility that his own dissociation in that moment is a reaction to what is experienced by the client. Why is he unable to access a self-state that has access to the affective, informational and instinctive information needed to understand the point of view of the patient? Is the patient's own dissociative process deliberately (if unconsciously) interfering with his ability to empathize? Stern says yes.

Leaning heavily on an inter-subjective understanding of the analytic dyad, Stern's description of concepts suggests that self-states are not simple one sided experiences (Stern, 2003), but are mutual creations. On one hand, they are attempts by two subjective others to connect with one another in the face of enormous difficulties. In another, they are in collusion, ever missing the mark as material too frightening to face is subtly suggested and then dissociated as quickly as it is sensed. From this point of view, Stern asks us to consider the inter-subjective field and the role that dissociation might play within it from one of the clearest vantage points. Like climbing a hill and standing on a rock in the middle of the brush after hours of hiking, one can finally see the forest through the trees, if only for a brief moment.

Why then would the patient (or any of us) "cordon off certain self-states from contact with others?" (Stern, 2003, p. 849). Reaching back to Sullivan and the concept of self-states, we are asked to remember that they are accessible only within certain contexts, even to the patient. If the underlying anxiety is too great, the fear of disintegration too overwhelming on an unconscious level, then dissociation is a predictable outcome. Protecting ourselves from a deluge of frightening feelings, memories and unspoken anxieties, we retreat. And, we are experts without knowing it. Like riding a bike, before we know it we are pedaling and we are three blocks down the road and on our way to safety.

"Dissociation is the unconsciously enforced separation or disconnection of the kinds of experience associated with different selves, a separation motivated by an unconscious discomfort, or even a sense of doom and dread, about certain kinds of experience being simultaneously known, sensed or felt" (Stern, 2003, p. 851). In Donnell Stern's view of dissociation, the patient is both aware and unaware. Perhaps addressing the speed at which these processes take place, Stern makes a profound point about context, enactment and dissociation and what they mean for any two subjective others attempting to reach a mutual understanding.

Enactment is the process by which we are attempting to write the wrongs. Each day we head out into the world with a quiet, unspoken hope that we can find a new way out, that we can right the wrong that was done to us in our frightening and traumatic past. We are looking for a message that the world is safe now, that the danger has passed. Like a double-edged sword, our own "self-systems" sabotage our attempts. Perhaps knowing all too well that the danger never truly passes, it works over time, keeping us ever vigilant, ever prepared to defend ourselves in whatever way we can. For many, that defense is dissociation.

We must be cautious to remember that the self-system is indeed us and just as we unconsciously seek new encounters with one cordoned off area of ourselves, so too does this other equally "us" part of ourselves shift ever away from that connection. The clinical implications here are profound. How do we approach our frightened yet connection-desiring patients without triggering the anxiety that will inevitably shift them into a self-state that feels safer for them? How do we demonstrate safety while asking them to remain in the state where the information lies? These are indeed

questions not easily answered.

Evidence in empirical/cognitive science

Trauma, Dissociation, and Conflict: The Space Where Neuroscience,

Cognitive Science, and Psychoanalysis Overlap

In the article titled Trauma, Dissociation, and Conflict: The

Space Where Neuroscience, Cognitive Science, and Psychoanalysis

Overlap, (Sommer-Anderson, S., and Gold, J., 2003), Frances

Sommer-Anderson (a colleague and kindred spirit of Philip

Bromberg, one of the leading voices cited in this paper) and Jason

Gold explore the considerable ground shared between neuroscience,

cognitive and psychoanalysis by describing a series of papers first

presented at the APA's Division 39 conference in April of 2002.

And of course, that ground is considerable. The article takes time to

explicitly state that there are those who do not see the utility in

attempting to synthesize theories form each discipline and also notes

that even among those who do there are significant differences in the

accompanying explanations regarding the overlap (Sommer-

Anderson and Gold, 2003). Still, they moved ahead to identify

commonalities.

And, of course there would be many. If the brain and the body

are the substances in which the phenomenon of experience are made manifest, then there are likely to be many physiological correlates to be identified by empirical study of the body and the brain. While we will never be able to point to an area of the brain and identify love, we can, using imaging technology, point to areas of the brain that "light up" when the person being imaged states that she is experiencing feelings of affection (Parasuraman, R., & Rizzo, M. (2007). Still, there is no inherent contradiction in suggesting that the experience is more than the sum of the body parts. One can never understand what it feels like to sit in first class on an Airbus A-380 sipping champagne on a transoceanic flight simply by studying aerodynamics or even working on its construction.

In this way, psychoanalytic theory can be considered a "rich description" of phenomena that have biological underpinnings and cognitive correlates but are usefully understood when symbolized and then described using language that is humane and experiential in nature. In fact, psychoanalytic theory has made many contributions to the empirical research in cognitive science and neuroscience by first describing phenomena that has been witnessed in the consulting room by listening to the voices of those they treat (Mancia, 2006). The relationship is a strong one and this paper holds that while the fields differ and that those differences will at times be vigorously (and even acrimoniously) defended when overlap cannot be identified, that nevertheless we have some obligation to continue to search for explanations for phenomena from each discipline as it informs the other.

Citing a case from the prestigious Rusk Institute (a progressive neurorehabilitation program at New York University that has historically sought common ground with psychoanalysis), Anderson describes a woman who was experiencing musculoskeletal pain (Anderson and Gold, 2003). "Ellen's pain had cognitive and affective components that for her, were inseparable. Stating that she was "dissatisfied with being anything less than Teflon", somatic illnesses would increase as a result of her unwillingness to pursue cognitions related to her pain. In essence, she had developed a fairly successful process of dissociating herself from the emotional residue of her pain. While she was able to keep her thoughts separate from her emotions, the consequence ultimately was an increase in physical pain.

Pointing to this as an example of mind/body dissociation, Ellen describes her traumatic childhood with an abusive father. Ellen had learned to tighten her muscles and to essentially "not breathe" in order to prevent herself from triggering rage that might come from her oppressive father. This terror/anxiety found a way to express itself however, in the form of muscular pain. The therapy in this case involved helping Ellen to explore those early experiences and to begin to return to breathing in response to threats of terror.

Her inability to experience triggering emotions was likely the result of the activation of an "affective core" that had "symbolic bodily and sensory components" such that as an adult, when Ellen was activated, her physical body felt the pain that her emotional and symbolic experience could not (Anderson and Gold, 2003, p. 537). Dissociation has consequences both in the inner emotional experience in a person but also in the body. Eventually, she was able to identify and integrate the fear and rage she had been dissociating and as a consequence, her physical pain was diminished.

In another insightful citation in the article, Gold works with memory in reaction to trauma. In an quantitative study, he attempted to identify dissociation in action by presenting stories to individuals. Half of the stories held traumatic story lines and half did not (Anderson and Gold, 2003). The result was that those who had read the stories that had content that was traumatic in nature had more difficulty recalling details of their stories than those who had read stories with more banal content. Impressively, Gold's simple study (which actually was intended to identify differences in personality style among those thought to be dissociative in style versus those who were not) was able to point to a common tendency among people to shift their attentional focus out of a narrative that is potentially threatening thereby reducing their memory recall of the story.

Citing and combining methodologies of narratives of clinical experience like Ellen's, a cognitive study on memory and traumatic story lines and ultimately a case study presented by Philip Bromberg, the authors of this study successfully illustrate how empirical data can aid in our understanding of trauma and dissociation by identifying underlying mechanisms and creating evidence for its existence as a phenomenon (Anderson and Gold, 2003). Undoubtedly, this evidence and overlap provide compelling evidence that these disciplines can contribute to one another's research and in the long run, be of help to our patients through enriched understanding by their newly informed clinicians.

Something Wicked This Way Comes: Trauma, Dissociation and
Conflict: The Space Where Psychoanalysis, Cognitive Science and
Neuroscience Overlap.

As this paper is first psychoanalytic in nature, it seems fitting
to focus more acutely on the paper presented at the conference by
Philip Bromberg. In his article, Bromberg opens with a memory
from childhood of a particularly nasty and predatory street cat named
Adolf who ultimately gets his comeuppance from a pair of birds who
were defending their nest full of chicks from his menace (Bromberg,
2003).

As the story goes, the birds gang up on the cat until he finally
collapses, frozen in fear. In language reminiscent of Peter Levine,
Bromberg muses about the potential reactions to a traumatic event
that the cat might have chosen and they included fight, flight or
freeze. Focusing on the freeze, Bromberg goes on to exquisitely
articulate a psychoanalytic explanation for this phenomenon using
psychodynamic, neuroscientific and evolutionary language to do so
(Bromberg, 2003).

In Bromberg's view, the cat's freezing response was analogous
to a dissociative response whereby in the face of psychic (and

potentially physical) threat due to overload, the cat found a way out in order to survive the ordeal (Bromberg, 2003). Citing an "evolutionary response" that enables survival in animals under threat, Bromberg states that this process "bypasses cognitive modulating" in humans and is more concerned with survival of a "sense of self" than pure biological survival as in the case of Adolf the cat (Bromberg, 2003, p. 559).

For survivors of repeated childhood trauma, the dissociative response of "freezing" in the face of trauma by finding a way to psychologically escape the threat is both a blessing and a curse. The blessing is obvious, psychic overload is avoided and the self is preserved (if now tucked safely away, split off, withdrawn and inaccessible by conscious processes) in order to live another day. The curse is more insidious. By "achieving his own self cure" the traumatized individual has now established a precedent whereby he may escape any traumatic or potentially traumatic event by withdrawing into himself (Bromberg, 2003, p. 559). Now, while an escape hatch has been created, the person can no longer remember salient details of the attack which sets him up to be on guard for potential trauma in the future.

The trouble is, the ability to distinguish between actual potential trauma and a mere triggering of fear of potential trauma is diminished. This sets the stage for what the DSM IV-TR might call (and what Bromberg actually does call) hyper-vigilance; an ever-present alertness to potential trauma (Bromberg, 2003). The title, Something Wicked This Way Comes (Bromberg, 2003) takes its name from this phenomena as described in Hamlet.

In a sense, the repeatedly traumatized individual now has established an "early warning system" that is poised to respond to trauma with this evolutionary gift of dissociation (Bromberg, 2003, p. 560). Overtime, as the stimuli that trigger this reaction is generalized, it now contains early glimpses of anxiety, behavioral clues in others, shame and even unidentifiable physiological responses in his own self system, the person is trapped by his own ingenious defense. The process will likely begin to occur without his knowing it and at incalculable speeds, shifting him out of the moment and into the dissociative realm where vital information that could lead to a different outcome are missed.

In severe cases, (personality disordered individuals and even those with Dissociative Identity Disorder), (DSM IV-TR, 2000), the person is completely at the mercy of his defense. Shifting rapidly from self-state to self-state in reaction to the most minute of triggers in order to avoid the threat of anxiety an integrated sense of self becomes almost unachievable (Bromberg, 2003). Here, Bromberg has made an exceptional case for an evolutionary process that has biological underpinnings that create greater insight into dissociation as a mechanism of defense for traumatized individuals.

Documenting this process in neuropsychological and neurochemical terms, Bromberg points to evidence that serotonin plays a large role in regulating this sensitivity that defines his "early warning system" (Bromberg, 2003, p. 564). Early trauma creates a decrease in serotonin levels which has a negative impact on one's ability to modulate arousal and so "produces hypersensitivity to seemingly mild stimuli".

This flaw in the serotonin system that is the result of the child's natural response to repeated trauma leaves the victim set up to be victimized in the future. If he is in a very literal and biological way disadvantaged in his ability to sense triggers and modulate his anxiety in response, his self system is likely to kick in, sending him into a dissociative state.

It is easy to imagine that, dependent on both innate factors related to genetically determined serotonin levels combined with repeated trauma (a stress-diathesis model understanding of the process) a person could be severely handicapped in the area of interpersonal relating. If one is constantly being triggered to withdraw, one is constantly missing critical pieces of information that could lead to different potentialities. Instead, he is over and over again traumatized. Around every corner is the abuser, waiting to strike. The body, exquisitely trained to avoid danger cannot be convinced that the danger is not there and does it's magic, resulting in a repetition of the trauma and the consequences that accompany it.

Having already described the process of enactment that underlies a person's tendency to repeat relationship dynamics in every new relationship using Bromberg's work and others, we will forgo repeating that now. In essence, this excellent article describes in bold psychoanalytic terms, using evidence provided by evolutionary psychology and neuroscience alike, describes familiar processes by which dissociation plays a role in maintaining past trauma as a going concern in the victim of repeated childhood trauma.

Back To The States: Victim and Abuser

States in Borderline Personality Disorder

If we have established that Borderline Personality Disorder is

in actuality a common consequence of early exposure to repeated

childhood trauma (Herman and Van der Kolk, 1987). Then, just as

we explored aspects of Complex Post-Traumatic Stress Disorder

then it seems fitting that we spend some time discussing the role of

dissociation in BPD. Elizabeth Howell, in her article Back to the

States: Victim and Abuser States in Borderline Personality Disorder_

(Howell, 2002) carefully explores how early trauma results in many

of the common dissociative symptoms that we have seen so far in

this paper among those diagnosed with Borderline Personality

Disorder.

In her work, Howell suggests that in the DSM-IV TR, "all nine

criteria can be understood as manifestations of a dissociation-based

disorder" (Howell, 2002, p. 922). Further, she suggests that a

"significant pattern of dissociated self-states in BPD" is

characterized by switching between masochistic/victim and

rageful/perpetrator self-states" (p. 923). These constantly vacillating

dissociated states, when used as primary mechanisms to modulate one's experience in the world, constitute the very definition of personality disorder. If she is right, then we must re-examine the concept of personality disorder (as Bromberg has suggested previously in this paper) as styles defined by excessive and pathological use of dissociation as a primary methods one employs to regulate affect in anticipation of the repeat of childhood trauma.

According to a study by Dell, 53% of outpatients diagnosed with Dissociative Identity Disorder are also diagnosed Borderline (Howell, 2002, p. 923). This comorbidity is highly suggestive of the the veracity of Howell's (and Bromberg's by means of deduction) suggestion that BPD is primarily a disorder defined by the use of dissociation as a primary and structurally pervasive style of interrelating with the outside world. The difference between the two, according to Howell, is that for those with DID, the dissociated self-states are mostly unconscious but for those with BPD, they are "consciously knowable but disavowed" (p. 924).

Like others we have read in this work, Howell suggests that repeated childhood trauma results in the creation and maintenance of separated and dissociated self states originated to serve the function of regulating the affect of a child in anticipation of anxiety (Howell,

2002). These self states fail to become integrated as they might in someone who is reared in an environment where there is soothing behaviors by the caregiver. The result is a child whose affect-laden self states are out of contact with one another and thereby are blind to certain types of new information as the person learns to vacillate between them, attempting to soothe the self like some kind of psycho-dynamic whack-a-mole.

In her model, there are two primary affective descriptions that apply to various self states. Those who emulate a masochistic identification with the abused child who cannot escape her captor and those that are identified with the aggressor whose connections to the child are not something that the child is willing to give up (Howell, 2002). According to Howell, a person can only identify with the victim self-state for so long without triggering the internal rage that was also associated with the abuse that she has suffered. Turning active into passive, the borderline personality disordered person takes on the characteristics of the abuser becoming ruthless, cruel and unrelenting.

Howell's descriptions of these two types of affectively tinted self-stares are reminiscent of DSM-IV TR's criteria for Borderline

Personality Disorder. In Criterion 2, the person must have a "pattern of unstable and intense interpersonal relationships characterized by alternating between extremes of idealization and devaluation". In Criterion 3, one is required to demonstrate "identity disturbance: markedly and persistently unstable self-image or sense of self" (DSM IV-TR, 2000).

Through a process of enactment, the BPD survivor struggles to maintain identifications both with an abuser and with her abused (Howell, 2002). As clinicians who have treated those with Borderline Personality Disorder, we recognize these vacillations that can occur with lightening speed. Dissociated from one another it is also common that those with BPD are unwilling or unable to recognize that there has been a vacillation or that there are differences between them. And with good reason. By dissociating these two major affective states from one another, the person is able to maintain separation between two inconsolable parts of herself: the part of her that is vulnerable to abuse and destruction and the part of her that is capable of perpetuating abuse and destruction. If she were to integrate the two, there is a risk of being destroyed. To let one or the other go, she risks losing attachment to the only mother she knows and the abused self that is her only real proof that she exists.

Howell's dividing of the many self-state experiences that are demonstrated by those who are diagnosed with Borderline Personality Disorder offers us a way in which to look for general trends in our patients and a way to further understand why and how thee states are so persistent and resistant to being let go. So powerful is the need to maintain a sense of self and to maintain ties to the caregiver, the self-system and it's underlying neuropsychological mechanisms will go to almost any length to preserve the self's integrity, even to the point of dividing that self into separate parts that lack much or any ability to recognize one another.

Memory Difficulties and the Shrinking Hippocampus

The hippocampus is a brain area that is largely considered to be an area that is, in part, a major player in the process of gathering sensory information and storing that information in long-term memory. While there are many processes that must occur over a period of time that will allow one to to covert a bit of "working memory", (which is largely a function of attention and concentration in the frontal lobes) to short-term memory and then into long-term storage for eventual retrieval, nevertheless, the hippocampus has a major role in the memory conversion process.

The process goes something like this: "When a memory is initially formed, the hippocampus rapidly associates this distributed information into a single memory, thus acting as an index to representations in the sensory processing regions. As time passes, cellular and molecular changes allow for the strengthening of direct connections between neocortical regions, enabling the memory of an event to be accessed independently of the hippocampus" (Preston, 2007).

If the hippocampus is damaged, memory is likely to be affected. Attempting to gather literature linking damage to the hippocampus to emotional trauma (which thereby might shed some light on the problems of amnesia and dissociation) a team of british researchers conducted a meta-analysis of existing studies on trauma victims who had been radio-imaged, establishing the link.

In an article published in the British Journal of Psychiatry in 2002, University of Aberdeen, Professor Alastair Hull conducted "a review of all functional and structural neuroimaging studies of subjects with PTSD" (Hull, 2002). He found that "The most replicated structural finding is hippocampal volume reduction, which may limit the proper evaluation and categorization of experience" (p. 106). Suggesting increased levels of cortisol (a natural hormone created in stressful situations) in the brain as contributing to the damage, we can begin to understand how the consequences can have physiological traces that may help us to understand what a client is feeling phenomenologically.

What this article's and (those it reviewed) findings seem to suggest is that emotional trauma causes biological changes in the human brain that inhibit one's ability to convert information to memory. Reminiscent of Donnel Stern's concept of unformulated experience, it is possible and even likely that there are actual physiological disadvantages being experienced by victims of repeated trauma. What we experience as dissociation may be directly tied to this reduction of capacity in the brain.

Challenges to Symbolization: A Dark Broca's Area

Another area that this paper has focused on with some intensity is the area of symbolization of experience through speech. We are able to communicate our internal thoughts and feeling experiences to one another and even to ourselves as we bring those "proto-thoughts" to the surface and convert them to full-blown thoughts by using our access to language as a way to organize that experience.

For those of us who have worked with traumatized patients, we are aware of a phenomenon that is related to dissociation wherein our patients are unable to find words to describe their heightened emotional experiences (traumatic events). Not resembling a defensive resistance to discussing their feelings at all, something completely different appears to be at work. Many times, the patient is eager to describe those experiences but is only able to access fragmented memories of the event and often, even when there are memory traces being felt, the patient cannot find words to express them, try as he might.

The results of a 1989 study involving the neuroimaging of PTSD patients found that an area of the left hemisphere of the brain called the Broca's area showed significant differences in activity than those of non-PTSD cases. The Broca's area "which mediates verbal communication and organizes problem-solving tasks into a well-ordered set of operations in a sequential fashion seems to be less active in people with PTSD" (Davidson, 2004). Here, we see a suggestion that there may be decreased access to speech making (and thus symbolization) capacity as a result of one's exposure to repeated trauma.

These studies, when considered together, seem to suggest that there are differences in the way that information is converted to memory and processed into language in people who have been exposed to trauma. The implications for analytic theory are striking. It may be that these studies and others like it are beginning to provide quantitative evidence to suggest what we (and our patients) have been experiencing. What appears to be happening is that dissociation as a defense to trauma may have biological underpinnings and learning to better understand how those deficits may affect our patients' ability to work with dissociated material could have a profound impact on how we treat trauma victims.

Conclusion/Discussion of Literature

This literature review has been an attempt to create a narrative of the process of dissociation as it contributes to a larger cycle of retraumatization as experienced by victims of repeated trauma. We have borrowed literature from the disciplines of psychoanalysis, trauma studies, neuropsychology and cognitive science in order to generate better understanding of what each of these important areas of study can contribute to our work as students of clinical psychology and eventually, as clinicians.

There are limitations too. This corpus of literature is not in any way a "state of the science" of what we know about dissociation. Each area of academic study from which we sought information has much more to add to the study of this process. One could write multiple volumes on the information and literature that was not included or even considered for this article. I have attempted to focus the article on specific questions while maintaining an open-ended spirit of inquiry and in that process there are of course, failures.

Additionally, the hermeneutic and logical methods of study that are employed by this paper and by many of the articles referenced herein are rejected by many in the academic community and for substantive reasons. Many of the articles (while rigorous) are potentially victim to confirmation bias, validity and reliability issues and general questions about the lack of quantitative data to support the claims made. With that in mind, however, this paper holds that there are multiple ways of knowing and hermeneutical discourse, clinical judgement and observational skills are just some of them. I have attempted to use rigor and empirical values in both the selection of the articles as well as in the construction of my own theoretical conclusions in order to avoid these pitfalls.

There are unanswered questions. While an attempt to be thorough and rigorous has been diligently attended to, there is much to be studied and learned about trauma and dissociation. Some of these issues will be raised in the results section of this paper, others will be addressed in the conclusion as I consider clinical implications and also areas for further study. Others will remain unanswered. Perhaps acceptance of that fact contributes to the success of this work and to the intellectual curiosity that will fuel the next one.

CHAPTER III. METHOD

Critical Review of a Body of Literature

This dissertation is an exploration of human experience as much as it is an academic inquiry into a given topic. The experience of trauma is a powerful phenomenon that is not easily described using empirical methods and so, in an attempt to grasp the experience of repeated trauma, the defense of dissociation and the frustrating, and frightening horror of living in a retraumatization cycle this paper turns to several kinds of literature in order to evaluate and describe the experience.

From one perspective, this paper is a critical review of a body of literature. Specifically but not exclusively, this work turns to current psychoanalytic literature in order to borrow from the vast clinical experiences and theoretical knowledge contained within its tradition. In selecting this body of literature, special attention was given to those authors who hold certain theoretical assumptions about the human experience.

A key element of the method of study in this work is the understanding that it is my goal to understand dissociative processes from the perspective of those who have experienced it and that is why this work relies so heavily on psychoanalytic literature. In many ways, it is the only research (aside from qualitative interviewing and possibly various art forms) from which one is able to get a "rich description" from the inside of the process.

Specifically, this work accepts that underpinning the development and maintenance of personality is an affect regulation, relational and inter-subjective matrix based on the relationship of one to the outside world and those within it. While it is true that there are many models of personality theory within psychology generally and without the psychoanalytic tradition. It is also understood that there are even those who do not accept that personality exists at all. This paper assumes the above mentioned model and begins its inquiry there.

Rationale for selecting corpus of literature

Within the relational model of personality development there are many theorists whose work stood out to this author in preparation for the literature review portion of this work. Authors who were found to be frequently cited in modern psychoanalytic literature were sought after to provide the basic theoretical tenants of this work. While volume of works cited does not necessarily guarantee that all of the work will be veracious and of good quality, each citation was carefully considered on its own merit in addition to its popularity.

Attempts were also made to evaluate the philosophical underpinnings of those authors in order to provide context for their developing models and theories. Additionally, authors and their works were also selected for the content of the work itself. As the paper began to take shape, I looked for psychoanalytic authors whose work was logically and philosophically connected to the work and it's attempts to better understand the phenomena in question.

Finally, work that appealed to the sensitivities of this author, his life and clinical experiences and his clinical judgement were selected for inclusion. As a student practitioner, I have had the privilege to be exposed to many authors, mentors and patients who have built and developed my skills as a scholar, clinician and observer of human experience. With this in mind, decisions and assumptions were made about which authors and articles to include and which to not include. Still, attempts were made to ensure that this process was completed with as much objectivity as possible.

Articles were compared to additional literature in each respective field in order to ensure quality and veracity throughout.

As technology increases, our ability to image and examine the physical body and correlate that information with phenomenological experience continues to increase at an enormous pace. With that in mind, in addition to psychoanalytic literature, this work includes relevant empirical studies from the domains of neuropsychology and cognitive science.

As is stated elsewhere in this work, the varying fields of psychology have much information to offer one another in order to increase our understanding of behavioral, cognitive, spiritual and emotional phenomena. As I prepared for this work considerable thought was given on how to include quantitative material without suggesting its superiority or that it was needed to act as a kind of ballast to support the other kinds of evidence provided. While it is not accepted that quantitative evidence is the sole standard by which all evidences are measured it is also accepted that various kinds of phenomena do not lend themselves easily to quantitative or otherwise reductionistic methods of inquiry, if at all, I do believe that providing quantitative support where possible adds to the power of this study to persuade and provide an accurate description of the process that has been described.

Addressing Intellectual Issues raised in the literature

Throughout the literature review, the results and the discussion portions of this work, intellectual issues raised by the supporting literature were addressed in the area of the paper near the citation itself. If there were logical conclusions drawn without additional support, alternative possibilities were discussed. Additionally, as unanswered questions were suggested by the literature or by the process of synthesis of multiple pieces of literature, attempts were made to draw conclusions that fit within the body of work as a whole whenever possible.

Process/Method for Systematic Analysis

Once the literature was gathered based on the aforementioned criteria, I set out on a systematic review of the literature. As the literature came from many unique kinds of sources, there were some differences in how particular kinds of literature were evaluated and analyzed. One cannot analyze an empirical study citing quantitative data in the same way that one evaluates psychoanalytic literature that is based on a combination of case study and the clinical experience of the author.

This work was driven in large part by the research question. As demonstrated early in this work, it is clear that the problem of retraumatization is a vexing issue for clinicians as well as for those who are victim to the process. With that in mind, this work set out to explore, in as open-minded an inquiry as possible, what factors might be involved in the maintenance of trauma as a ongoing concern.

To that end, I repeatedly returned to the research question and my own hypotheses in order to answer a fundamental question: "how does this piece of literature contribute to the explanatory power of this work in the area of dissociation as a process involved in retraumatization?" In determining how to present the works that were studied and in determining which components were not useful, this question served as a guiding principle. In this way, I attempted to make this work a coherent discussion of several points of view that shared common rhetorical and clinical themes.

This paper is meant to promote understanding of a complex process by gathering information from disparate sources that had not been gathered together before. Analysis was intended to synthesize these various sources into a common conversation regarding the topic. While in some cases, for example, a neuroscientific writer may not have been explicitly attempting to find a physiological correlate for a given psychoanalytic concept or description of experience, it was my attempt to identify how this given study might alter or further our understanding of a that phenomenon.

The bulk of the literature selected for inclusion in both the literature review and discussion/conclusion sections of this work are psychoanalytic in literature. With this in mind, it was my attempt to identify modern pieces and authors that were relevant to the work. As I repeatedly returned to the research question, I would look for ways that the article in question contributed to my own understanding of the process under consideration. Pieces that were not relevant, lacked citation in other work or otherwise were not in step with the modern consensus in psychoanalytic thought were not included.

Additionally, each piece was evaluated within the context of the parameters established at the outset of the study. I was looking for descriptions and explanations that were relational in nature.

There are excellent psychoanalytic sub-areas that may contribute to this particular question but those authors were not considered for this work.

When evaluating the quantitative literature that was considered for this work, in addition to the criteria that must further the understanding of the question it large, additional constraints were applied. Studies were evaluated for various types of validity as is considered standard in empirical research (Kazdin, 1998), for the power of the statistical analysis and for its general recognition within the scientific community. In this way, how often a given author, study or series of studies appeared in other bodies of literature influenced the weight that was applied to it in this study.

Another kind of material that was used in this study might fall into the category of "books, anthologies and collections". As much of the work in the early stages of the literature review moved beyond the journal article phase and have made it into various books both by the author herself and by others attempting to create textbooks and "state of the science" articles, it was important for me to establish some criteria for inclusion and review. Material from books and other combined sources were analyzed for their contribution to the exploratory nature of the study as well as for its own value of synthesis of the work.

For example, I often turned to writings by Mitchell and Black (1995) whose work is highly distilled and accessible. With this in mind, I considered the material in their work against other literature that I had discovered in order to establish veracity and reliability of conclusion with other authors. If it could reasonably be established that the language, as printed, seemed to be confirmed by my own interpretation and the consensus of other thinkers in the field, then it was included and that language would be used in my own synthesis.

The resulting work (this dissertation) is an attempt to find a common language between these multiple fields within the larger discipline of clinical psychology. Psychoanalytic theory, neuropsychology and cognitive science all offer unique points of view that add to a larger discussion of this particular problem in psychology. This dissertation makes an attempt at synthesizing these diverse voices into a clear and coherent description of the phenomenon of dissociation as a major contributor to the troubling problem of victims of early childhood trauma maintaining a vicious cycle of retraumatization.

Summary of Review of Literature

_____The goals of this work have been to further the understanding of the complex and dynamic process of trauma, its sequela and its powerful grip on those who have experienced it. In order to do that, a thorough literature review was conducted, critically analyzed and then synthesized in what hopefully amounts to a theory-making endeavor. Standing on the shoulders of giants, I hope to bring my particular voice, experience, knowledge and wisdom to the table in order to make this an original contribution to the literature.

Of course, this treatise falls short of its goals in many ways. Psychological phenomena is a tricky thing to study. In the 100 or more years that it has existed as a formal discipline, the language used to study it, the prevailing theories and the basic understanding of human experience have changed many times. Going back and forth from scientific observation, phenomenological inquiry to case study and others in research cycles that are always creating new questions and theories, the changes continue. This paper has attempted to embrace that always shifting method of inquiry in order to employ methods in hopes of generating a description of phenomena that can be known in many different ways.

Of course, there are many other epistemological ways to gather awareness of and information about any given phenomena. This paper is not comprehensive in that way. I have selected a type of exploration that lends itself to discovery based on my own interests and style of study and description. As a consequence of this work, it is hoped that new questions are asked, greater understanding of the frightening experience of retraumatization is promoted and new methods of helping the victims of trauma are considered.

CHAPTER IV. SYNTHESIS AND DISCUSSION

Within a Relational/Inter-Subjective/Affect Regulation Matrix

Trauma. At the heart of this paper (and much of what Clinical Psychology in general attempts to study, understand and heal) is an attempt to better comprehend precisely what is happening, in psychoanalytic language, as a result of trauma in general and as a consequence of dissociation in particular. When one is impacted by trauma, he has had his relationship to the outside world severely challenged by betrayals of his sense of safety, belonging and competence as a thriving human being; threatening his very sense of self.

Humans are relational creatures by nature. Empirical evidence has been gathering for decades in support of a fully relational explanation (within a context full of allowances for innate factors like temperament, intelligence, physiological uniqueness, etc.) for human personality development. We have learned that our closest relatives in the mammalian world will not only suffer emotional consequences of a failure to attach to a caregiver, but also biological and physiological ones as well (Harlow, 1959, Goldson, 1989). We also know that critical brain areas do not develop correctly when a person has had a failure of attachment as a result of neglect, abuse or worse (Debellis, et al., 1999).

When humans are traumatized, the brain area known as the Broca's area which is largely responsible for the creation of speech, fails to develop to optimum capacity, leaving the person literally at a loss for words and a diminished capacity to fully articulate their experience to other humans (Davidson, 2004). Further, we know that hippocampal damage as a result of emotional trauma impacts memory formation, leaving the victim at a disadvantage when it comes to storing and recalling critical information about her traumatic experience (Hull, 2002). These missing links, in the form of amnesia, can leave a trauma victim without the ability to fully grasp and make meaning of her experience, a pivotal process in helping a person feel connected to her community.

These and other key brain activities that are impacted by trauma underlie the personality development of human beings and these impacts, while barely detectable by even the most modern imaging techniques have far ranging consequences in the phenomenological experiences of a living person. If one cannot recall her traumatic experience, she is unlikely to learn what happened in an accurate fashion, and what to look for in order to prevent it from happening again.

As a result, she is trapped in it's wake, forever grasping for breath, because for her, trauma is everywhere. From the perspective of one's role in community and how we understand how vitally important one's support system can be in determining the final impact of trauma (Herman, 1992), if one cannot speak, one cannot tell her story to her mother, sisters, friends and others to get support and to be freed from her isolated struggle.

In the construction of this paper, we are looking to understand better the role of many different processes with a special emphasis on dissociation. We have take as a given that one consequence of trauma (in very human terms) is that quite often, a vicious cycle ensues. As defined by Davies and Frawley (1991), our cycle includes dissociation, projection, projective identification, reintrojection and retraumatization as phases not necessarily occurring sequentially but as key processes experienced repeatedly in varying order in order to create a cycle of traumatic re-experiencing that is such a vexing thing to heal.

For this author, dissociation is not only the first phase in the process of retraumatization, it is involved with all phases of the cycle and it is quite possibly the most impacting when considered within a relational context. Once we have accepted that a relational matrix underlies the very essence of living for humanity, we must accept that a breach in human relations that reaches the level of a traumatic experience is going to impact the very foundation of the way that a traumatized individual relates to others in her life. If, as a result of early and repeated trauma, our victim retreats into the interior corridors of her cognitive, emotional and existential self (Fairbairn, 1952, Guntrip, 1971), her ability to relate to others in a satisfying and mutually gratifying way is going to be severely hampered, perhaps to the point where relationships are of no comfort whatsoever.

Nearly without exception, in order to develop fully (both psychologically and physiologically), a person's world must first be safe and reliable (Winnicott, 1964, Goldson, 1989). One must feel that she can step away from the caregiver and explore the outer world for ever increasing degrees of satisfaction and fulfillment. An ideal (or even Winnicott's "good enough") caregiver has through countless repeated lessons, taught the young infant that her love is protective and is strong enough first to survive the infants destructive tendencies and ultimately to protect her from threatening forms, images and symbols in the outside world.

If our growing infant continues to feel the world is safe enough to explore, her security-seeking operations now sated, begins higher pursuits in her relationships in the outside world than some measure of success has been achieved. Natural and optimal exhibitionism and libidinal curiosity drive the person further and further into the outside world, occasionally returning home to the mother for encouragement and further reassurance that the outside world is safe, that she is strong enough to handle what may come at her and that the internalized caregiver is still accessible in spite of the growing physical distance that now separates them (Guntrip, 1971; Sullivan, 1953; Winnicott, 1964).

In the case of our traumatized infant, nothing could be further from the case. She has been betrayed. Her caregivers, whose duty is to demonstrate the safety and security of the outside world, have failed. The world is not safe, and in fact neither are her caregivers. They are either the source of her pain, or silently complicit in it, or both at least from the child's point of view. They have either terrified her or failed to protect her from the terror. In either case, they are not strong enough to keep her from being being threatened or destroyed. They are internalized as monsters or weaklings or both. And what the self internalizes, the self becomes. When one has not internalized the caregiver as safe and powerful, one is unable to internalize the world or even the self as safe and powerful and in response, her only option is to retreat.

Retreat is a logical choice. When an infant has no power to win on her own, she cannot fight. The world is cold, it is hot, it promotes hunger, anxiety and even terror. The infant has no power, no ability to challenge it's ultimate destructiveness. Without the learning that a safe relational context provides, the infant is at a loss, at the whim of every destructive force that she encounters. Retreat is not only a logical choice, it is the only choice. The alternative is a frightening unknown full of monsters and demons who seem bent on her destruction. While we are speaking metaphorically here, we must remember that when we consider the experience from the perspective of the child, the monsters are very threatening and quite real when the fear of annihilation is real and an actual anxiety in her mind.

As we have learned, dissociation takes many forms. For some, there is banal or everyday dissociation which is merely a lack of attentional focus and is in fact a normal psychological process (Stern, 1983). Each day, we are bombarded with stimuli, some harmless like the trees in the forest and some threatening like the city bus barreling through a yellow light as we scurry across the wide avenues on our way to the next venture. While our attentional focus is not required for us to stroll quietly through the nature center, at peace with ourselves and the world around us, it is essential in the concrete jungle where large and fast moving objects hold sway. This differentiation process of what is potentially dangerous and what is not in order to decide where to put our attention is essential to survival and to our forward movement as humans.

While we may not think of this as dissociation, we don't do so perhaps only because of it's implicit and accepted functionality. We all are grateful that we are not being overwhelmed by the stimuli that we encounter on a daily basis. if we were, we could get nothing done, we would be forever caught, like deer in headlights, looking for danger at every turn, never able to quiet ourselves enough to connect to others, to love them and to receive their love. We would be too busy fighting for our survival to make such relationships possible.

In addition to surviving in the physical world, the basic process of dissociation as defined as "unformulated experience" by Stern (1983), also helps us learn to survive in the relational world as well. As humans, we learn how to thrive in relationship by learning who to trust and who to avoid. When positive relational experiences define our early developmental phases, we come to learn that our instincts are trustworthy and that others in the world can mostly be trusted and that you will know when they are not. This system which Sullivan considered to be the self system when functioning optimally, allows us to see the forest through the trees (Sullivan, 1953). We know that we are safe and so others become something to seek out as sources of emotional satisfaction, of fulfillment and of love. For those who have been traumatized, this same self system is on overdrive unable to turn itself off and allow for higher pursuits.

While this primitive psychological process is likely necessary for our survival, if used by a developing psyche as a primary coping strategy for dealing with a harsh and oppressing world, the consequences can be dire (Stern, 1983). Instead of being an attentional selection process that allows one to go about her business, rightfully unafraid of the world and it's inhabitants, it becomes a distorting procedure whose function becomes one of primary affective regulation. Here, pathological dissociation is a primary method utilized by a traumatized psyche to find relief from affective overload.

For the traumatized individual, the world is not safe. She is not equipped to handle the challenging situations that life presents and so she has retreated, perhaps learning the art of self trance or perhaps she has simply learned that escaping to a fantasy world deep within her psyche and out of the outside world will temporarily reduce the terrorizing tension that being in relationship to the outside world inevitable promotes (Herman, 1992). A tension so fundamental that all persons encountered in that world have the potential to recreate the fear and torment that initiated the process in the first place.

This affect regulation procedure employed through dissociation may have temporary benefits like allowing the person to successfully deny what is happening to her in the middle of a rape, a beating or even during a mild berating but the in the long term, the consequences are ultimately destructive (Bromberg, 2003). In the words of a traumatized male patient whose father was in the habit of waking him with a pistol to the temple once told me "I learned how to be a crazy person in order to stay sane when my dad was crazy but now that my father is dead, I'm just crazy". For this man, dissociation was a way of life, he could no longer trust anyone, he was constantly waiting for the other shoe to drop.

While the leap from dissociation in the form of retreat into the psyche might seem like a huge hurdle to overcome from a hermeneutic point of view, from a phenomenological one, the process is easier to understand. If we think back to our physical world example and imagine the careening bus once again, we can imagine what a disadvantage one would find herself in if she were unable to keep her eyes off of every road sign, car, streetlight or passerby. If, in reaction to those stimuli, her response was to retreat from the world out of fear that it were essentially ordered to be against her (in spite of it having no personal bias against her whatsoever) the world would suddenly become a very dangerous place, much more dangerous to her than for the other pedestrians on Broadway.

Without the ability to accurately screen what is dangerous and what is not, we are at the mercy of the world around us. A bus is not in itself dangerous, in fact to many, it is a life-giving mode of transportation. It allows them to work, to visit friends and to seek out medical care when needed. It has no ill will. In the same way, when others around us are not able to be screened out as either helpful or harmful, benign or malignant, they all become a potential source of danger. In it's very essence, dissociation denies us information.

As we will later explore when we delve further into the mechanisms of enactment, projection and projective identification, dissociative processes stand in the way of the traumatized person receiving accurate information about others. When one dissociates, there appears to be no separation between them. They are all triggers of the generalized belief that the word is ultimately frightening.

While in the case of a natural selection process of stimuli it allows us to focus in on what is potentially harmful, helpful or necessary and to disregard the rest. Unformulated experience in this way of thinking, is neither good nor bad. It is simply experience that has not received attentional focus (Stern,1983). When the process of dissociation becomes so prevalent its defensive operations are universally employed, the unformulated experience becomes the key information that has been denied.

For my male patient with the angry and threatening father, all of the men in the world were not only like his father, they were his father. Threatening, and in his mind, ultimately biased against him, every man he encountered was a threat. As a child, he dissociated whenever his father went into a rage. Eventually he was simply moving in and out of various dissociated self states all of the time just to keep up with his father's moods. The result was an inability to discern what was real and what was imagined. It all became one. Generalization of the internalized object relationships had occurred.

For this man, it was not a matter of simply looking for overt cues of aggression that would send him into a dissociated process (Sullivan, 1953). The human relational system is so attuned to others that the slightest cues can be discerned. For most of us, a change in a person's inflection or a shift in the shape of a person's smile merely elicits sympathy, empathy or concern. For one whose entire self system has come to be defined by dissociation, slight shifts in expression or tone are experienced in rapid fire succession as a cue to a threatening series of events. These events are ultimately interpreted as dangerous regardless of any actual meaning intended (or unintended) by the real other in the encounter. Once this process is in place, she is left at a major disadvantage when it comes to experiencing relationships as positive phenomenon. She has not developed the capacity to differentiate between them.

Often, this dissociated material or "unformulated experience" is made up of specific, factual events of one major trauma due to an amnesic response in the moments adjacent to the incident, but in the case of victims of repeated trauma, the story is more insidious. What has been dissociated, or unattended to, is not merely a factual event (no matter how frightening or terrifying) but all of the cues that the dissociative process has begun. For the chronic dissociator, the she does not know that the event has happened. In addition, she is not aware that the triggering process has been initiated or that a shift to a new self self-state has occurred.

This process is well illustrated by a dream that a patient of mine who was a victim of repeated sexual abuse by series of cousins and then ultimately by all three of her brothers. "I dreamt that I was asleep and all of these snakes were crawling all over me. Suddenly, I realized that I was sleeping and when I woke up (and I was actually still dreaming) I was actually swimming in a beautiful lake and I just thought that the water was snakes. I suddenly started drowning and I couldn't get out of the water, I was terrified of the water even though moments before I was swimming perfectly".

In this dream, expressed during a session a week after she had told me that she was molested by so many relatives, I believed (and she agreed) that the initial swimming event was when she would first dissociate in order to deny the sexual encounter and calm herself down. The second swimming event (where she felt like she was drowning and that she had forgotten that she knew how to swim) was a metaphor for how the repeated sexual abuse had left her unable to tell what was safe and what wasn't. She had even forgotten about the things that she knew full well how to do.

While with any dream interpretation there is room for disagreement, the client embraced the concept and resonated with its implication that her great skill at dissociation had left her unable to tell who the bad guys were, and so, in response, she had begun to define all those around her as potential violators and she could not be in relationship at all. Each and every relationship that she had attempted to build, beginning in early adolescence, had ended with either the other person unable to handle her constant accusations that they were taking advantage of her or actually became victimizers of her in one way or another.

Dissociation had robbed her of her ability to feel safe in relationship. She had become so sensitive to slight changes in the inter-subjective field between her and the men she loved that she interpreted everything as a potential assault, missing any information that might be interpreted in other ways.

This generalization process is at the heart of the retraumatization process (Stern, 1983). For the victim of repeated trauma, the relational world is not a safe place. For those who have been brutalized, sexually abused or verbally destroyed by a needed caregiver, there are few moments where one can relax into love with their partner. In reality (and in phenomenological terms), she is forever unable to be in relationship with an actual other.

The powerful imagery of her introjected objects supersede any ability of the actual other subject to redefine the relational prospects. In fact, there are no real subjects, as the Object Relations theorists might put it, there are only introjected objects, frozen in time (Fairbairn, 1952; Guntrip, 1961). The details of the subjective other are so frightening and trigger so many barely understood or even recognized past events that they are avoided altogether in a dissociative process so refined that Sullivan's term of "suave" is an accurate and even soothing way to describe the process (Sullivan, 1937).

If we think back to Jessica Benjamin's observation (1990) that recognition of a truly subjective other is a developmental milestone, we can see how challenging this is for a person who has either been betrayed by a caregiver or abused by one. Dissociative processes appear to supersede developmental ones. If one is unable to learn to be in the world safely without fear of destruction and annihilation, one ceases to mature in profound ways. One never learns the benefits of a loving touch, a nurturing kiss or the soothing qualities of a bear hug. If each of those are events that may result in her death, she is hypervigilant. She must ward off the anxiety that is experienced when she is approached by an "other", and dissociation is a highly successful method employed in order to stave off this material.

In fact, the tension created by subjectivity in the part of an other is so overwhelming that for many, there really is no such thing as intersubjectivity. Rather, she lives in an ever-shifting landscape of hyper-emotional reactions to triggers so subtle that they never reach consciousness, they remain sub-cognitive and in the realm of the primary or even reptilian level (Bromberg, 2003). The frontal cortex never stands a chance. So triggering is the thought of another who cannot be defended against that there very existence is denied. My patient, the male whose father had the gun fetish, put it this way: "it's like I never met another man who I couldn't predict was going to try to kick my ass". In the end, he was right since his dissociative processes frequently ended up with him in bar and street fights.

Intersubjectivity may be the ideal way to understand human development from the point of view of an observing psychologist but it is the ultimate threat for the traumatized individual. Without access to vital information, one cannot recall that father was only one man who could not be trusted and that all men are not the same. One cannot slow down long enough to hear his intentions if one does not know that he has already projected the entire relational contents of his relationship with his abusive father onto this unsuspecting but potentially dangerous other. One cannot afford surprises or afford to take the risk that this time things will be different if one has already made the decision that this is not possible; that all men are evil and that there is no such thing as a safe other.

The dissociative process makes way for projective processes to have their field day. Like Bill Murray in the movie "*Groundhog Day*" (Murray, 1993), many traumatized individuals live the same day and the same relationships over and over again. There is no such thing as a lover, there is no such thing as a friend, each becomes a representative of the past. While they may or may not all actually be evil, they all can be converted to devils through dissociative processes. And after all, the devil we know is much better than the devil we don't know.

Enactment

The re-enactment process is one of the vexing phenomena known to humankind. Freud himself pondered why it was not of greater concern to analysts given it's frequency of occurrence. Each of us has spent time with a loved one who has spent a lifetime in bad relationships defined by lack of mutual affection, neglect or even abuse. We heartbreakingly listen to sad and sometimes terrifying tales of these relationships hoping that this time, our friend will see that the pattern appears to be destructive to them and to be the source of so much misery and finally put a stop to it. As clinicians, we know even more. We as clinicians are acutely attuned to minute suggestions of relational repetitiveness and we watch our clients cultivate major insights into their patterns only to come back in six months having begun a new relationship that to us, feels identical to the last, even in its infancy.

What drives us to repeat the tragedies of our past? Why do we love those who do not love us, abuse us even try to kill us? There are, of course many ways to consider this phenomenon. While we have come to some understanding about how dissociation plays a role in preventing us from noticing that the smoke has cleared and that not all others are exactly the same as those who have traumatized us. We can even explain this to our clients, as if a simple explanation (even if framed as a sensitive interpretation) to help someone think differently is enough to redirect a person away from a life pattern that has literally defined their relationship experiences from the very beginning of their lives.

Object Relations theory has much to suggest about the enactment process. In the world of internalized (and more importantly) introjected objects (accepted here as a substitute for actual, subjective others) there is little room for novelty. In fact, it is avoided at all costs. Novelty has proven itself to be frightening proposition filled with dread, anxiety and potentially, physical danger. The introjected object is by it's nature, a frightening object. In the words of Fairbairn, "there are no good objects" (Fairbairn, 1952).

In many ways, we might consider the object internalization process as an evolutionary gift. Memories of frightening others serve to allow us a new way of combatting potential danger in our midst. From an evolutionary point of view, as might be suggested by Peter Levine (1997), we have been given a way to remember dangerous situations in order to reenact them in our minds so that we can potentially escape sometime in the future if a similar situation presents itself. Additionally, because the introjection process so indelibly imprints the frightening object into our mind, we are not likely to forget it or the potential cues that could serve as ominous warning signs in the future.

For the traumatized individual, the challenge is that all or most of the people she encounters will eventually become bad objects due to her primary identification with her abusers and there will be few good interactions to interrupt the introjection process (Fairbairn, 1952). Inside the developing psyche of the traumatized individual there are few safe people to provide images of strength and security which she is able to internalize as a part of herself. The bad objects, of course come to define her experience. Once generalized to include most or even all others, the bad objects come to confuse her, preventing the world itself from taking on a benign or even benevolent tone.

These internalizations are now the very definition of relationship. And moving forward, long after the actual people who came to define those object representations have passed, she is still unable to move beyond them as the generalization process has so come to cloud her view of the world. It and all of those who dwell within it are scary beings who have her worst interest, in mind. From this vantage point, the re-enactment process has little to do with compulsion and all to do with how the world has actually worked for her.

Our memories of others often serve to prove to us that we are loved and actually support our libidinal drive outward, toward the other. For the traumatized soul, the anti-libidinal processes have so come to dominate the inner workings of her psychological mechanisms that the psyche is constantly in retreat, back toward the bad object representations. Occurring unconsciously, she is unaware of the insidious process that drives her back to reliance on those old objects, every relational trigger reminding her of her trauma; her past life. In fact, without those triggers, she is lost and can feel nothing at all.

For those who have ever asked a close friend the question "why do you keep dating all of those jerks?", the answer to that question comes into clearer focus when we come to understand the underlying essence that the very idea of human relationship has been defined by terrifying people and the terror they inflict. What started out as an evolutionary gift to enable one to be prepared for danger has now gone haywire in the chaotic environment of trauma. Everything is danger and in fact, the only way that one is able to recognize that the other (or even her own self) is even present is if she is triggered.

While on the surface, this suggestion may seem counterintuitive, it is only so if you attempt to distance your thinking from the profound impact that trauma has on the developing, relational personality. When one approaches an "other", one is looking to feel, to be acknowledged and to have their experiences validated. The lack of the validation is equal to a lack of existence (Bromberg, 1993). If one does not feel one does not exist and if one does not exist, neither can the other. While this debate may seem philosophical, when considered from a phenomenological perspective, it's tether to real life becomes clearer.

A female patient of mine who came to the clinic where I was working because her boyfriend was emotionally abusive came to a session crying. "He called me a whore", she said. "I've never been with anyone but him and he still calls me a whore!". As we processed this painful interaction she went on to have some insight into this relationship. "I should I have known", she said. "From the first night, he reminded me of my dad...just the way he talked". When I asked she meant, she said "on our first date, he told me that I was an angel, the prettiest little angel he ever saw". That was what her father had said to her repeatedly, often with remorse on evenings after he brutalized her mother in front of her. "He actually made me feel just the same way my father did".

While it may not be clear if it is true that he was able to quote her father word for word as she described, what was most true about this interaction was how much she resonated with her idea that he made her feel like her father had. In other sessions, when she told me of men who had approached her in the past, she had often stated that she couldn't picture herself with them and that was why she had rejected so many seemingly good men. For her, she literally did not exist unless she was feeling the trigger that this man (and other, even more abusive ones) was able to make her feel.

When one is traumatized, needing to feel alive is an essential part of being in relationship. When one is dissociative as a matter of course, much of existence is lost to amnesia and inattention. For those who learned the art of self-trance, the threshold for feeling alive is higher than for those who have not had to escape into the psyche in order to survive. In this way, the traumatized individual must be reminded of those objects or else her world does not exist. She is instead, lost in dissociative mechanisms (Herman, 1992).

Another significant feature in the relationship to the object world of a traumatized person is the actual relationship to the objects themselves. As described earlier by Judith Herman (1992) and others, the traumatized person is a victim. Too weak to fight, to vulnerable to survive the dangers or running away. And so, a deal with the devil is made. The caregivers, no matter how frightening, are needed. One cannot live without those who feed, provide warmth and offer the pittance of evidence that one is alive and functioning in the outside world. One needs as much of this as she can get.

Here, we have another potential glimmer of light that can be shed on the vexing question of why so many traumatized people stay in relationships that for all intents and purposes are so damaging to them. While there are many dangers associated with forming a relationship with someone who is potentially dangerous and damaging on both emotional and physical levels, it is far less dangerous than not existing at all. For my client who could not be in a relationship with someone that she could not picture herself with, the risk she would take is to continue to exist rather than to disappear.

This point of view is a challenge for a non-traumatized person to wrap their head around. The anxiety associated with non-existence is but ubiquitous and subtle and can be a motivating force for all kinds of defensive reactions. It is really understood best when considered from the point of view of the trauma victim with a conscious awareness of and an attuned sensitivity to the frightening history that has been experienced.

As we have seen, our very existence is dependent upon recognition. Whether distorted or not, the traumatized person has formed her internalized objects based on actual relationships and in those relationships, she existed. For those of us who have not been so traumatized, our recognition (and thus our existence) does not come exclusively from these frightening internalized objects. It comes from a subjective experience of subjective others. This luxury is not affordable to the traumatized person.

In the chaos of a traumatizing home the tension between needing to be cared for and needing to protect oneself from the caregiver is such that the growing psyche is dependent upon the subtlest cure about how to behave. As described by our previous article, the woman who was plagued with bodily pain because of childhood trauma that left her holding her breath so as not to provoke violence, recognizing the other's minute changes was essential to her survival (Sommer-Anderson and Gold, 2003). Unknowns were threatening and could lead to very serious consequences.

In this atmosphere, the child is not free to enjoy the world, accepting novelty and invention as it came along. She must be ever aware and able to predict what will come next so that she can be certain that tonight she will not be raped, beaten or worse. In this way, she does not exist without them. Like a prisoner who needs the watchman who holds the key to the prison door, the victim of repeated trauma is in need of her keepers, without them she is likely to wither away and die, this is at the heart of why she must remain in contact with them.

While an adult or even adolescent survivor of repeated trauma may not appear to "need" the caregivers in her life to survive, the damage is already done (Herman, 1992). As we have seen, the traumatized individual does not live in the "actual world" the way that non-traumatized people do. Hers is an internal world that is under constant surveillance. Vacillating between dissociating out of the external world and into the fantasy world where she is able to predict the behaviors of dangerous others and back into the physical world where her pain, fear and anxiety is so overwhelming that retreat is once again the only option, there is little time to make a permanent home in the outside world.

In may ways, the internalized objects are more predictable than the real ones. In her mind, if she is quiet, holds her breath or otherwise is able to change her behavior in order to calm the adults she needs so intensely, she is likely to remain alive. To rely completely on the unknown quantities of the outside world is to rely on nothing at all. That world is entirely too unpredictable and too dangerous.

The result here is a person who in many ways cannot exist in the outside world for long periods of time. The dissociative tendency to retreat works so well that it becomes over-learned, the only way to live at all. Living in an internal world means living in a world of internalized objects. And for this reason among others, many victims of repeated trauma stay inside, dissociated away from all that is scary about the outside world. Once again, the devil she knows is far better than the one that she does not know.

Here, we are better able to understand these constant re-enactments of past traumatic relationships. So powerful (and yet extremely subtle and even unconscious) is the recognition of her own aliveness through the enactment process that in spite of all of the pitfalls, even for relatively high functioning, self-reflective and otherwise insightful clients, it is often preferred to releasing herself from the pull of those internalized objects. If they are not triggered, they do not exist. If they do not exit, than she does not exist. This is the dilemma that our traumatized clients face when we ask them to break their dissociative cycles and join the world of truly subjective others and their unpredictable behavior.

Dissociation is an activity that is essential to our understanding of the re-enactments that contribute so powerfully to the retraumatization process. As we have already explored, dissociation is an internalization process, in many ways it is the opposite of living

in the outside world. When we dissociate, we turn away from what is

happening in the external world and we turn toward a place deep

inside ourselves where we are safe in our fantasies of control and of

mastery.

While losing a parent is a challenge to any of us, loosing the

parental internalized object is devastating to the traumatized

individual. Life has been defined in relation to this internalized

object. The pedophile father is controllable in the fantasy world, and

his daughter exists, for all intents in purposes, only in relationship

with that internalized object and the self-states with which it is

identified. When one has grown up believing that the outside world

is something to be savored, one is able to live in the outside world

and in relation first to the parents as others and then to more and

more subjective others in the outside world.

This results in a natural individuation process that allows one

to access and be accessed with all manner of others. When one has

not learned that the outside world is safe, the inside world is the only

refuge and the only place where one exists. If the internalized objects

that define these internalized worlds are threatened with annihilation (which is precisely what we are suggesting our clients to do in psychotherapy) then we are threatening them with annihilation as well.

The process of maintaining trauma as a going concern rather than as a relic of a challenging and frightening past is understood more clearly when we, in psychoanalytic terms, begin to describe the actual, living phenomena of the psyche in a relational and inter-subjective context. Whenever two people come together, a new inter-subjective field is created and must be navigated. How we respond to that field is largely defined by the earliest and thus most important relationships in our life.

Our patients who are traumatized and thus dissociative in many ways are not living in the literal world that we would encourage them to inhabit. Their world is defined by internal experience as defined by a frightening and chaotic past. In order to help them to gradually shift from the inside to the outside, we must first understand what life is like on the inside. If survival is dependent on that world, our goal of reducing reliance on that world must be preceded by an understanding of its rules, its "homelands, it's seasons, its songs of its own" (Hunter, 1973).

The creation of and reliance upon an internalized world with parental figures who are manageable, are less frightening and provide needed love and nurturance does not happen overnight an neither should we expect our patients to relinquish it easily or without a tremendous conscious and unconscious struggle. In fact, learning to utilize dissociation is a creative act and we must learn to understand and respect our patients for choosing to accept and learn to live in spite of incredible odds.

In fact, if we were, in our imaginations, to liken the fear that our clients experience when they are faced with the proposition of giving up the only world that they can live within as similar to us giving up our own parents, our homes, and our own lives, our ability to understand and identify with the experiences of traumatized individuals is likely to greatly increase. And only by learning to understand this world which we ourselves find so threatening, from the point of view of those who have to live within in do we have any hope of helping our clients reduce their dependance upon it.

Projection

The process of maintaining trauma as an ever current and likely future event in a traumatized persons life is clearly a complex process that involves many important subprocess that occur both consciously and unconsciously. We have noticed here, for example that many aspects of dissociative experience are completely unconscious and many others appear to have conscious or cognitive components as is the case with self trance. The unconscious vs. conscious dichotomy may seem over simplistic and even grotesquely dualistic as a mechanism for psychological experience but it is important that we recognize that we are talking about the experience of traumatized individuals who have not been provided the same integrative capacities that many people who have not been traumatized often easily enjoy.

If you are raised in a home where there is little integration between experiences, where anger is not a matter of escalation but is experienced as a "zero to sixty" kind of phenomena, then the experiences are not symbolized as gradual increases or reductions in tension. Things are either tense or they are not; dangerous or benign. If you are raised in an environment flooded with alcohol and drugs, mood shifts are far less predictable after three shots of hard whisky than they are in a home where temperance and moderation are molded.

In the same way, if your caregiver suffers from bipolar disorder or has a borderline personality organization, the on and off switches are unlikely to be readily apparent. The same is true if you are raised in a home where the dark of night, after you have slipped into deep sleep, is quite possibly the scariest time of day. Being woken up in the dead of night by a perpetrator who inflicts emotional and physical pain before threatening to kill you if you tell anyone what has happened is unlikely to lead to integrative tendencies. In fact, we know from sound empirical research that victims of trauma are hard wired toward hypersensitivity (Howell, 2002). If you cannot control or even manage your affective reactions to stimuli, intellectually considered reactions are out of the question.

When we think about projection in these dichotomous terms, we are now better able to consider how this defensive process works for traumatized individuals. Projection, in many ways relates to phenomenological experiences of the inside and the outside the self and to the "other". For a traumatized individual, these distinctions are often experienced in black and white. Like Melanie Klein's (1932) splitting mechanisms, there is good and there is bad and they must always remain separate. In fact, if they are to become mixed together, the result is unlikely to take on characteristics that appear integrative. They are likely to feel confused, disorganized and even frightening.

This is the case with projection. In many ways, projection is a result of the inability to discern internal experiences from external ones. As we described earlier, for the traumatized person, learning to live in the internal environment in response to a near total lack of a perceived locus of control is a survival tactic with frightening consequences. In projective processes, one is unconsciously triggered by seemingly conscious external events that are quickly translated into internal and unconscious ones.

The person in the external world is not fully experienced as a true other by the traumatized other as she lives in this internal world where a relationship with internalized object representations takes precedence over the actual external ones. In fact, it is easy to speculate that the triggers occur so frequently and with such velocity that one is constantly being triggered outside of her awareness. Each word, each change of expression and each threatening gesture are distorted by dissociative processes that disable the person's ability to continue to relate in the external world. She is simply over stimulated. And so, as is habit, she turns to the internal world for comfort.

These triggers are so powerful and her unconscious faith in her ability to handle them in the real world is such that she is unable to tolerate these warded-off, dissociated and unwanted emotional stimuli. For the traumatized individual, the external world and all of those who inhabit it carry unthinkable potentialities of death and annihilation. If one has learned to survive these threats through self-trance, dissociation or even fantasy, turning inward is the only thing one has learned to do in the fact of threat. And so, she projects.

When one is projecting, it is as if one is having a dialog with the internalized object representations rather than with a subjective other. A severely dissociative patient of mine, in a group setting once said "I feel like all of you are looking at me like I am a freak. I am totally afraid of all of you right now. It makes me feel like my brothers did when I was a kid... Whenever they would notice me, they would tease me and say the meanest things...Then like they were just hating me more and more, they would attack me...All three of them at the same time...Every day was a nightmare." This woman was actually learning to symbolize her previously unformulated experience. In weeks prior, she had been having intense reactions to the group and simply walking out.

As we have considered several times in this paper, introjected objects are not simply loathsome creatures who the person had a simple hatred for or even a fear of. While they may have traumatized their victims, they are often the most needed people of all. This is why projection is such a powerful defensive process for traumatized individuals. When one is projecting, one is no longer separated from those members of the family who were the only family members that she was given. She has, in a sense, brought them back to life.

While it may seem easy to wonder why anyone would want to bring terrible abusers back into the future from the past but as in the case of enactment, projection is a mechanism of keeping those others and thus herself, alive. It is essential when thinking about victims of repeated trauma that the sense of self is ultimately more fragile than we are typically used to thinking. Traumatized individuals are made to feel as though they do not exist at all other than as servants to the observer and so as life passes, in order to remain in existence within their own conceptualization of the world, they must have access to their perpetrators.

If we consider this point from a "Sullivanian" perspective and think about his use of the term "self-states" within what we would now think of as an inter-subjective field, we can understand these concepts a little more clearly (Sullivan, 1953). Each of us is constructed not of one single, unitary whole but of a composite or amalgamation of self states experienced in succession. In fact, our self-states are the primary way we know that what we are feeling, what we know and even if we are feeling. In fact, they help us to know if we really exist at all.

These self states (that we know are affectively tinged and contain their own knowledge banks, their own access points to various memory systems) within the self always exist in relation to others (Howell, 2002). In fact, there is no self when there is no "other". Each day, as we go about our business, we interact with store clerks, cab drivers, school children, loved ones and even frightening others who wish us ill. As we make contact with each of them, a new inter-subjective field is created, generated between the two of us, half them, half us. It is not an overstatement to suggest that we are not simply composed of our own selves, we are at least half constructed by the process of experiencing an "other".

For most of us, the self states that we experience are fulfilling and novel events that are based largely on the actual interaction that we are having. The handsome boy who rings us up at the coffee shop makes us feel good in part because of who we are, in part because of who he is, and in part, because of who our brother was, our cousin was, our high school crush was or even who someone we can't even recall was. The interaction creates how we experience both him and our own selves. The degree to which we are able to access the actual moment may say something about the degree to which we are able to tell our inside experiences from our outside ones.

For a highly traumatized individual, the boy behind the counter may not be the handsome brother who was always kind and stood up for her at school. He may be her frustrated and sexually predatory brother who raped her in the dead of night. He may be the frightening older cousin who spent the summer on the couch as her babysitter by day and perpetrator by night. If he was, he is much less likely to be experienced positively by the traumatized individual. He is likely to trigger her in many unconscious ways, causing her to shift into self states that have access only to vaguely intimidating emotions, reduced memory recall or even paralyzing affective reactions.

Like all dissociative processes, projection is the desperate attempt of the self-system to manage triggering events. If a person is being unconsciously triggered, she is likely to project onto that person the characteristics of the internalized object representations in order to return to the self states that brought her some measure of comfort and tension reduction during an earlier and more frightening time in her life. While using the term desperate may seem unnecessarily harsh, it carries with it all of the urgency one needs to fully understand the experience that this process involves.

Traumatized individuals often live on a razor's edge. Without being aware of it, a traumatized person is now standing in front of a perpetrator who may have inflicted unspeakable psychic or physical pain. The person, who moments ago might have been a new friend or boyfriend is likely to have little or no awareness that he has just been transformed by the unconscious of his new loved one, just like her. So rapid are these shifts that one is given to lash out, to react just as one might have done to her perpetrator.

During this process, the buildup of tension is so great in the trauma victim that she will do anything to escape them. One method of discharging that tension is to project it onto the unsuspecting other who is now standing in front of her (Fairbairn in Guntrip, 2001). The trouble is, as we all know, lashing out is only a temporary solution. Even among those who are not traumatized, projection is a common defense that only temporarily makes us feel better. Perhaps we illicit anger from our new projected-upon other or perhaps we become aware of what we have done and now feel even worse. Either way, the pain has only temporarily subsided and ultimately we will have to confront it sooner or later if we are to get past it. Projection and dissociation are terribly short-lived analgesics.

Now that we are on the subject of the others who are the receivers of our projections, it is important that we now consider the impact of the powerful and frustrating dissociative defense of projection. When we consider that there is, in fact always an "other" involved in our projections, those of us who are able to function in a world filled with actual "others" are forced to confront the painful realities that actual "others" do not enjoy being projected upon. In fact, for most people who fall victim to this process, they greatly resent it and will likely react negatively to the process.

Projection has a profound impact on those who receive it. As therapists, we are very familiar with patients who, when triggered, reach ferocious volume when they scream at us, call us names and threaten to leave treatment. And those of us who have ever taken a lover who is plagued with tendencies to project onto others can speak fluently on the feeling that one experiences when a simple, even loving movement goes terribly wrong and without warning, we are turned on with a vengeance. We are often frightened, angered and almost always, confused. What have we done to receive such wrath? Are we really that bad of a person that we have hurt this other so much? Are we really so insensitive that we do not have the simple awareness to notice how mean and hurtful our words are?

Among the many reactions to projection that those who become the recipients of it have, it appears that there are two that stand out as categorically definitive. One one hand, there are those who likely are not trauma victims themselves and are not seduced by the projection process. They are likely to abandon the projector due to the anger they experience when being accused of something that they have not done. On the other hand there are those who are more likely to have been traumatized who find the projective process unsettlingly familiar, who respond to it the way old sailors who were unable to resist the call of the sirens did. Drawn inexplicable toward the craggy shore, these men crashed their vessels into the earth, losing them to something they could not explain.

For those who do not respond to the projection and find it, for lack of a better word, kind of crazy, escape is their highest priority. Like a kind of unspoken mating ritual, the projectively-defended trauma victim sounds a tone like a dog whistle, heard only by those with ears to hear it. For those who are unaccustomed, the sound is not beautiful, it is bemusing, confusing and frustrating and the result sends them heading for the hills. Those who can experience the "other" know that they could not be as cruel, as thoughtless or as insensitive as he is being accused and they have nothing to gain from maintaing this escalating frustrating tie to someone who does not seem to truly recognize them.

Projection serves to help traumatized persons maintain ties to those internalized object representations that they need so desperately. When the "others" who refuse to accept the invitation to be projected upon leave, the are weeded out and while the immediate result is painful for the projective person, she has successfully identified someone who will not help her to maintain her needed ties to her once-essential perpetrators and to the self-states who are able to access them. Like the dance of various birds on a nature television program, some are selected to join the dance and others not. Most often, we are unable to discern what has defined the selection process but somehow, even unconsciously, the birds know. Such as it is when projection is used as a litmus test for a suitable lover by a person whom victimization has left with no option but to use whatever she can to keep herself from being destroyed.

And then, there are the others. Like the birds who cannot resist the bright red bellies and rainbow plumage of our rare birds captured on a nature program, these are the souls who are drawn ever closer to those projections, as if they have seen them before, or possibly even lived them before.

If we accept that we are proven to exist in our own minds by our relationship to the others we encounter, than it is not so hard to imagine that we are looking for exactly that kind of affirmation in our lovers, our close friends and in our non-biological family systems that we create in school, in college and in our overall social lives. For most of us, we are recognized as others and we recognize the others in our life in ways that while being a blend of projections, introjected objects and actual encounters in ways that are challenging and frustrating but ultimately satisfying and encouraging. We build on that mutual recognition and create new experiences together that further cement the bond.

For traumatized individuals who rely primarily on internalized object representations as a way to know that one exists, one must have those representations continually triggering them into various self-sates that remind us that they are alive. The best way to ensure that the process will continue in a way that will validate our existence is to look for a response from our potential mate or friend that indicates that they will play ball. We are looking for someone who will become that projected other.

A male patient of mine who had grown up in a multi-family household that was patrolled by a jealous and overbearing male patriarch who had a sexual interest in the young boys in the flock described his adult relationship with men (he also turned out to be gay) in a way that places the projection process and what it ultimately seeks in a context which makes it particularly clearly understood. "Every guy I meet either dumps me a few days after we start dating or he sticks around and six months later, I'm throwing his IPod out the window after he tells me that I'm fucking crazy...It's like half the guys know I'm crazy and bolt the moment they notice, and the other half know to but they stick around just long enough to torture me".

The projection process is neatly described by the young man I just described. What he seemed to know instinctively is that projection is just one part of a two part process. While there are many functions that projection serves, including tension reduction, maintenance of ties to internalized caregivers and perpetrators, one key function is it's ability to set up the "other" in the encounter for the defensive process best suited for a reciprocal response to it: projective identification.

Projective Identification

Dissociation is a process of self-enforced lack of awareness or consciousness of stimuli, memories, self states and of course, accurate perception of the "other" in an inter-subjective context. As we turn the corner in this work from the role that dissociation plays in the maintenance of trauma as a current event and future prospect within the intra-psychic landscape of a traumatized individual, it is highly relevant to pause here and recall that taken for granted within the hermeneutic framework of this study are certain tenants that were described at our outset.

Among them (and probably most importantly) is that the literature reviewed within this work draw us closer and closer to the conclusion (or at least comforting assumption) that in order to accept a relational framework as the underpinnings of personality one must accept that an inter-subjective perspective implies that at least two subjects are involved in dynamic and mutually influencing processes (Benjamin, 1990). When one is able to recognize that oneself exists, this knowledge must occur in reaction to an "other" in order to constitute a separation of the self as construed as an object within the perceptual field.

Within this self-other dynamic is a mutually created field of shared (although not wholly) experiences and more importantly, perceptions. The dynamic is established in infancy and likely before as the infant and mother slowly separate from one another first as the fertilized ovum separates from her body and shifts into her uterus, eventually being forced out of the body by the mother's intrauterine wall contractions during labor and then slowly and more progressively as the child begins to recognize that food, comfort and love come from outside herself, from the other who she is ultimately dependent upon.

This slow recognition process is a natural part of the separation process between infant and mother which is the ultimate template for self and other in relationship. In many ways, this formative and yet primitive individuation process is the building block of the relational model of personality and how this process proceeds will ultimately influence most (if not all) other relationships entered into by the infant as she progresses through childhood, onto adolescence and ultimately into adulthood (Winnicott, 1960). The process is affectively tinged from day one as anxiety, comfort, joy and frustration are passed back and forth from mother to her child as each person slowly comes to accept her ultimate (if not complete) separation from the other (Sullivan, 1953).

With this is mind, we must accept that trauma too is ultimately a relational phenomena. It is in relationship with our caregivers that we are most often first traumatized in both big and small ways.

While it may seem that there is no such thing as a small trauma, it is necessary to recognize that the individuation process will almost always contain some amount of trauma. All infants will ultimately experience anxiety and possibly even terror at numerous points along the road as they become aware of their "aloneness" and separation from their mother.

Hunger will creep up on the infant in new and more threatening ways once the child has been birthed into the new world. Cold and hot temperatures, loud voices, upset stomachs and stinging diaper rashes will all send subtle messages to the child that she is not always safe and satisfied and that she will not always be comforted as quickly (or at all) as she would like. These experiences are not simply physical events, they are interpreted by the child. Her aloneness is threatening and potentially overwhelming. Without cognitive methods to self-soothe, the infant is at the mercy of the mother and even worse, at the mercy of the elements in this new solitary world (Klein, 1930).

Melanie Klein (1932) was the first to discuss the process of projective identification as a defensive process that is initiated by the infant in order to help her manage her anxiety in the face of a frightening world. The infant must, in some way come to terms with her fear of annihilation in this lonely world. In fact, it is too overwhelming for her to even contain within her own intra-psychic space and so it must be expelled. And expel it, she does, directly into her closest other, the one who is responsible for her survival.

In Melanie Klein's view of projective identification, the anxiety experienced by the infant is too great to be contained and so it is thus "expelled" into the mother like waste products were in the womb environment. That way, the infant has not lost her self completely and these materials are projected into the mother; still accessible on one level to the infant's consciousness but at safe enough distance so that the child no longer directly feels the direct blow of her overwhelming fear that she will be destroyed. The mother then, has become a part of the infants fantasy of herself. The bad feelings that she has once experienced within herself are now a part of the mother.

The mother, now in many ways becomes the fantasy object that the infant has experienced and this can, in turn, have unintended consequences. The mother now, has become part of the frightening object relations scheme of the infant. She has now come to take on characteristics of the infant's deepest anxiety at the world: that it will cause her unspeakable pain and ultimately destroy her. The mother now has the enemy within her. The setup here is now a frightening proposition for the infant. She now needs the very frightening projected object that she has attempted to expel from herself. While the initial attempt may have been made in order to allow the mother to experience what her affective response to the world may have been in order to elicit a necessary response from the mother, the product of the projective identification process has far more dire consequences for the infant in the long run.

While the infant who receives the ultimate care and concern and affection and comfort needed from the mother may come to tolerate the projected material in herself and thus begin to relate to others without the projected material being at the center of the relationship, the traumatized infant has no such comfort. For her, the projected material is now in the mother who is her first "other" but ultimately it is within all others as the object relationships become introjected and the infant begins her process of generalizing the experience of the first other onto all others to come.

As we imagine this process in adult victims of recurrent trauma, we can imagine how relationships with others will become clouded with the projected unwanted material that was initially expelled. If she experiences others primarily through projection, projective identification is likely to follow which may cause a sequence of events to unfold in the relationship based on how the projectively identified other begins to experience the material that is now projected into her and the person who has projected that material in the first place. Here, we begin to see how projective identification turns the corner from being a relationship between one subject and her internalized object relationships and into one that involves an actual living breathing other; even if she cannot actually experience that other as such.

When an adult survivor of childhood trauma has come to regularly employ the defensive maneuver of projective identification as a primary method of relating alongside our previously described process of projection, we can see that the process has both pros and cons for the trauma victim. One such pro is that the person is now able to experience herself and the others in her life in ways that she might not be able to otherwise.

Projected material, while unwanted may be thought of as being in safekeeping. By projecting the material into the mother and in this case the "other", one is able to access the material and the self-states that accompany it, later on. When a person has accepted (likely through dissociative process of his own) the projected material, he is now able to respond to her in ways that triggers her internalized object representations. She is now able to access, as an adult the material and the self states that created it. She is once again alive and thus relating to an external other albeit through pre-existing object representations.

As we have noted earlier, unpredictable relating to others is a tremendous challenge to traumatized individuals. They have grown up learning to separate themselves (through dissociative processes) away from frightening experiences and nothing is more frightening than those experiences that they cannot control. For many trauma victims, self-trance, dissociation of self-states and affective distancing are techniques employed in order to avoid affective overload (Stern, 2004).

If the process is not unlearned, it is likely to remain a primary defense mechanism throughout the lifespan. By continuing to utilize projective identification as a method of expelling unwanted and frightening material, the adult trauma victim is continuing to allow herself access to the self states that she has cut off from herself. Those self states and the introjected object representations attached to those self states are possibly the only way that she knows that she is alive.

Projective identification can be seen in this way as a method of recognizing her aliveness and thus lessening the sting of her fear of annihilation. Further, when the "other" experiences that material as within himself, his reaction will likely stimulate something in her that she is likely to recognize, and find familiar. And while it may be frightening in its own right, it is still the devil she knows.

The projective identification process employed as a defense her fear and anxiety becomes one more arsenal in her repertoire agains affect overload. By maintaining this process, she is able to continue to feel that she exists, that the demands of the world have not overwhelmed her to the point that she is unable to withstand it. By using projective identification in particular, she is now able to experience some distance and thus some control over this anxiety.

From the outside, it may seem like an obvious distortion of relationships with others. For those who were not traumatized, we hope that each relationship is new and unique, full of curiosity and wonder. We are not terrified by the unknown as we were soothed in our early time of fear and thus, the world is our benevolent oyster. To the psyche of the traumatized soul who is split of from her observing ego and thus from the awareness of a true other, those processes that seem such a delight to us must be warded off and one way to do that is to utilize projective identification as a defense.

On a final note on the process of projective identification and the experience of it from the perspective of the one who is doing the projecting, we must remember that maintaining one's most privately held beliefs about the world is essential to feeling safe in it. To the traumatized person, the world is a frightening place filled with monsters, demons and "others" who mean them harm and they are potentially around every corner. So integral is this unconscious belief system to the maintenance of a sense of self that it must be protected and projective identification allows her to do that. When she projects onto a willing participant, her "other" is likely to respond in a way that confirms her beliefs about the world and at least one function of projective identification is to do exactly that.

While we have been far from comprehensive in this discussion of the impact and experience of projective identification on the person who is doing the projecting, so far, we have barely scratched the surface in our discussion of what the experience is like for the "other" in the scenario. What of the person who has unwillingly or unwillingly participated in the projection/projective identification pair process? In fact, their response is essential to the maintenance of the process as defensive measures with effective results.

As we have stated in the projections section of this work, the projection process serves as a kind of litmus test for the trauma victim. If she is successfully able to project onto the person her internalized object relations, she is able to determine if a suitable match has been found. In much the same way, projective identification also allows one to find out if one will confirm her beliefs about the world, if one will trigger the dissociated self states and their internalized object relations and if one will contain her unwanted material at all.

For an non-traumatized person, receiving unwanted material from an "other" who you have entered into a relationship with is very likely a disorienting experience. You have begun the process of opening up to the other person, you are beginning to become more and more vulnerable and allowing him to experience more and more of your inner thoughts and your inner world. The process is exciting and while challenging, you want nothing more for it to continue as love is made in such ways.

Suddenly, the person is reacting to you in ways to do not recognize. Have you done the awful things to this person that he says you have? Are you threatening to abandon him? Are you threatening to overwhelm him? Are you reading his mind? While your first guess is no, you have come to trust this person and his words so you give him the benefit of the doubt. You may even find yourself acting in ways that you never imagined yourself doing.

Many may never get this far, spotting the projection right away and cutting their losses and running the other way. For others, they will go just so far and then will find an alternative route out the back door. For the trauma victim who is now in relationship with a projecting trauma victim, the process may be all too familiar. If he is indeed a victim of childhood trauma, and he has now agreed to stick around, there is good reason that the very processes that are experienced by the projecting other are now occurring in him.

While this paper is not a study in personality styles and is not suited to discuss with great detail all of the particulars of the behaviors, emotions and beliefs of all trauma victims, it is reasonably safe to say that trauma victims often find each other and when they do, the stage is set for the retraumatization process to begin in both individuals. If one's reaction to the experience of another's unwanted (and thus projected) material is to engage the material in his own dissociative process, the result is likely that his unwanted material and introjected object relationships are being triggered as well.

By interacting with the frightening material, he is able to access his own dissociated self states, his caregivers and the control that he has sought in his own life. The trauma victim who becomes actively involved in a projective identification process is no longer alone, he is back in the world, returning to engage in the processes that compose his defensive reactions to his own fear, anxiety and dissociated material. He is in fact, alive.

Just as the trauma victim who projects his unwanted material onto others is attempting a re-enactment of dissociated material in order to experience it at a safe enough distance to control it, so too is the person who engages with the projected material able to experience something similar. By accepting the material, he is able to maintain his attachments to his caregivers and ultimately to his self that is quite likely dissociated away from his own conscious experience and felt only on a vague and emotionally distant plain that is brought into focus when he engages this frightening material. His long-lost self states are desired and longed for just as those of the projecting trauma victim are.

Additionally, projective identification allows one to turn passive into active. If one is triggered and he begins to react to the material with aggression and even hatred he has found a way to control his warded off traumatic experience if only temporarily. He may be able to take revenge on his own abuser, access the parts of himself that are identified with a childhood threat or even enact a process that allows him to feel some level of control over his intra-psychic landscape that may be a chaotic place filled with insecurities, anxieties and other frightening emotional states. From this vantage point, there is much to be gained by engaging in a projective identification process with an "other".

As we can see, the processes of projection and projective identification set a person up to continue the cycle of retraumatization. If one has been able to successfully trigger the dissociated and frightening material, object representations and self states in one's self or in another, one has been able to enact some measure of aliveness, is able to relate on some level with needed caregivers and to safely experience material that is too frightening to experience with her own self. Is one is able to stir an "other" to act in a projective identification process in a way that confirms one's beliefs about the world (even disturbing and unconscious beliefs) then one has verified her existence by experiencing it in the other and safely expelled the unwanted material from her own body. He has made contact with the outside world and with himself but it is safe. It is no longer unfamiliar and scary, it is eerily familiar and thus better than the unknown. And while this process is ultimately a dissociative process with little conscious attention focused upon it, it none the less achieves the desired affect.

Reintrojection

The retraumatization process as described by Davies and Frawley (1999) is one defined by several stages that while not completely discrete or necessarily sequential are nevertheless identifiable with enough specificity as to be actual phenomenon. We have also seen that among the phases as described initially (dissociation, projection, projective identification, reintrojection and ultimately retraumatization) dissociation seems to have the greatest amount of overlap between them. We have seen that dissociative processes can be witnessed as a part of every phase, and reintrojection is no different.

As we have seen, projective identification sets one up perfectly for reintrojection. Through the use of projection, a victim of trauma has been able to recreate past experience with internal object representations without conscious awareness of the process. Through the projective identification, unwanted material has been placed inside of the "other" in the interaction creating a safe access point for the trauma victim to experience the material separate and outside of the self (Klein, 1932). While initially, the process may have served a function of allowing an other to experience the frightening discomfort of the infant, and elicit needed comfort, the process also has unintended and potentially unwanted consequences.

When one takes in the projected material of the trauma victim who is doing the expelling of the material, one is very likely to experience that material within themselves and is quite likely to have a reaction to it based on their own internalized object relationship experiences. The reaction to that frightening material may be to disavow it, may be to embrace it or it may be to react to it with the kind of anger and hostility that may have caused the traumatic events to occur in the first place. For example, a mother who was unable to handle her child's vulnerability due to anxiety about her own, may have treated the child poorly as a way to expel and discharge her own unwanted experiences. In the same way, if the adult trauma victim finds himself in relationship to another trauma victim who has a similar reaction to his vulnerability, he may react to it the same way the mother did and retraumatize the poor soul.

Here, it worth considering the role and purpose of introjected object representations in the first place. According to Fairbairn and Guntrip (in Guntrip, 1971), the point of the introjection of objects comes from the ability or inability of the infant to handle frightening emotional experiences. If the infant is terrified by an "other" he is unable to stay present, to confront the object and defend himself from the perpetrator of the terror. So frightened is the infant that he must find a way to escape the wrath in order to guarantee his survival. The intense vulnerability of the infant (both physically and in terms of ego strength) leave him at the mercy of others and so he cannot stay in a conscious relationship with this other.

The introjection process allows (or forces) the ego to split off from itself in order to find a suitable place to withdraw. Sending the ego inward allows one to disappear away from the danger at least in terms of conscious experience. Splitting of the ego, in the moment is an act of desperation fueled by intense anxiety and fear of annihilation (Guntrip, 1971). In many ways, the introjection of objects is the first dissociative act. While certainly unconscious activity is occurring long before this (even before birth) the introjection process is potentially one the first times that the unconscious mind deliberately shifts its attentional focus away from the outside world in an attempt to manage an affective response to an outside stimuli.

The introjected object, now a greater distance away from the conscious ego is on an unconscious level less powerful than it was before at least in the preverbal mind of an infant in the midst of early terror. The process may be protective in this way but it also has the unintended consequence of separating the infant away from not only the other but from himself, the ego is now split (Guntrip, 1971).

Another consequence of introjection of objects is that it potentially may serve memory functions. If a person is able to commit the affective response to memory (even unconscious memory) then he may be better able to avoid that stimuli in the future (Levine, 1997). There may evenbe an evolutionary undercurrent to the process in that it may be advantageous to introject a representation of a person and his response to you in order to better avoid it in future. If the trauma and the subsequent introjection were relatively infrequent than the person may have more emotional distance from a terrifying stimuli which may allow him access to better mental processing in the future. He not only may be better able to see it coming, he may be better able to prepare a proper defense.

While speculative in nature, this theoretical possibility may hold promise for future research. It also aligns fairly neatly with other work studied in this paper earlier on. Peter Levine (1997) and his evolutionary explanation come to mind as does Bromberg (1993) and his vicious cat Adolf. At this point, the focus of this paper is not on the evolutionary advantage of those who have successfully learned to introject so I'll return to the subject at hand which is the consequences of the introjection process.

While occasional introjection of objects may have had helpful functions for the personality, frequent or regular traumatic insults certainly have consequences. If the person is regularly traumatized by others in his life, the result is likely to be a pattern of introjection of objects. As the person develops in a traumatic environment, the likely response is further ego splitting and more dissociation. As more and more objects are introjected, fewer and fewer "others" are actually experienced as fully other "subjects" who can safely be encountered. Further, more and more relationships in the outside world are conducted in that world but now come to exist only as interactions with internal object relationships.

The trauma victim cannot afford the risk of relating to others who could potentially be dangerous in the outside world. He has learned, through good (or bad in all actuality) experiences that most others are dangerous and must be avoided and so, he turns inward where the objects are more predictable and to the unconscious mind, ultimately safer than those in the outside world. That world of others has come to be mistrusted and the split ego cannot tolerate the kind of affect over-stimulation that it presents.

The traumatized personality is one that is defined by internalized object representations rather than by openness to the experience of relating to others as subjects to be experienced on their own terms. The internalized representations serve the personality by keeping the ego safe but it also keeps the ego from accurately observing what is happening in the actual world and is caught up in cycles involving projection, projective identification and now reintrojection of those old objects.

As we have seen, the projected material has now moved from inside of the trauma victim to being inside of the other who has become projectively identified with it. He is now capable of his own reaction to that material and the potential to retraumatize the person is now fully established. Once the projectively identified person begins to respond to the material, he is capable of triggering the person with that reaction. And that consequence is at the heart of reintrojection.

The internalized object representations, as we have stated previously in this paper are not only associated with "others" that one has known over the course of a lifetime, they are also associated with dissociated parts of the self. These "self states" which we have come to think of as cut off from the observing ego and also cut off from other self states are now potentially triggered by the person who has projectively identified with the unwanted material. When those self states and the dissociative processes are triggered, the reintrojection process gets a foothold and causes the person to re-experience the affective states that triggered the introjection process in the first place.

This traumatic re-experiencing, sometimes consciously (but mostly unconsciously) causes the traumatized person to maintain and strengthen his tendency to split away from the observing ego and away from the outside world. The original purpose of the introjection was to separate one from affective states and the person triggering them through behavior that is frightening to the trauma victim has now been reconfirmed to the unconscious mind. The ego has no safe place in the outside world. While neither party is likely aware of this process, the object has now become reintrojected with a new face on it.

An additional consequence of the reintrojection process is that the unconscious belief system of the trauma victim has now been reified. All relational interactions with the outside world are potentially dangerous and must be avoided if annihilation is to be prevented. This confirmation of beliefs is repeated over and over again as each time the trauma victim encounters another who projectively identifies with the unwanted and frightening material responds to that material now inside him with sadistic and potentially retraumatizing consequences.

In fact, often the trauma that is triggered is just as terrifying as the original trauma. A patient of mine who has spent most of her adult life in and out of repetitive and painful relationships with men described her experience with introjection quite eloquently. "My brothers did it first but then it seemed like every guy I met did it too. It's like there is something I am doing without knowing it that says to them "you can rape her, she deserves it and she ain't gonna do nothing about it neither".

When the reintrojection process has taken hold in a relationship, old patterns are confirmed and relationships are moved further and further away from conscious processes. Each person encountered becomes just like The ones before it, only the ability to access them in the real world gets more and more remote with each passing relationship. Reintrojected objects now have multiple faces and now those multiple faces contribute to the belief that relationships are fundamentally unsafe.

Relationships are now moved to a safe distance for the ego of the trauma victim. By moving inward, away from the outside world, the person has protected herself from the affective overload that he is convinced will overwhelm and destroy him. The self system seeks safety and security first and a person who has learned to split and shift the ego inward has done so in order to seek safety and distance from the frightening other. The self system however appears to be a creature of habit and once the process has become reified through decades of reintrojection, one finds himself stuck. He is unable to experience relationships with subjective others because he is frightened of them, but he needs those others in order to know that he still exists.

Actual others have now become nearly impossible to experience. Each new face that he encounters now feels as if he is only wearing a mask over the dozens of other faces that have come to traumatize him again and again. In this way, the perpetrator has now become a regular fixture in his life. In fact, he is unable to escape him as each new person triggers the same unconscious, dissociated material that he at once would like to forget but at the same time allows him to maintain the needed ties to past caregivers and to his very self.

Reintrojection is possibly the descriptive phase in this process that shifts one closest to being retraumatized. The ability to stay present, in the physical world within relationships becomes a greater and greater challenge with each passing reintrojection. New faces are now no longer new faces to the unconscious, as the process of projection now may even come sooner in new relationships as the triggering process occurs with fewer and less stimuli than in the relationship before it. When one has reintrojected most or all of her past relationships they are now defining hallmarks of her own personality.

In this way, trauma is now a going concern within the life of the victim of repeated trauma. He now relates to all subjective others as if they are synonymous with introjected objects of the past. To the unconscious mind, there is no mistake. Others who do not trigger are either left or or not recognized. All that it can see are the myriad faces of the past, like a nightmare lived every time that the eyes are closed. New relationships now parallel the original traumatizing ones.

The process has other victims as well. While we have been talking as for this paper's sake as if there are neat categories in these relational patterns for one projector and one projective identifier. Nothing could be further from the truth. In fact, in relationships where the triggers have been strong enough to bring the two people together for any significant length of time generally involves two trauma victims, and two people who have the potential to reintroject the object.

Very often, the adult abusers of the now-adult trauma victim are themselves persons who have experienced unspeakable relational transgression. As we have described earlier, turning passive into active is a component of symptomology in adult victims of repeated childhood trauma. While our natural sympathies lean toward those who appear to be the victims of physical abuse, the perpetrator is quite like a victim himself. He too, is beholden to his internalized object relationship. Like dancing, the two interact unconsciously with their old relationships under the guise of new love. The new relationships now parallel the old ones.

Reintrojection sets the stage for trauma to be maintained as a current feature in the adult life long after the actual perpetrator is out of the life or even gone. So powerful is the need to maintain ties to the caregiver or even the self states that once related to it that the unconscious will live with the consequences of being regularly traumatized if its existence can be verified through the cycle. Reintrojection leaves a person set up with greater and greater potential to experience trauma in the adult life.

While we may have written about reintrojection as if it were the final stage in the process that it is not completely accurate. It is most expedient to talk about processes such as these sequentially in part due to our lack of a full understanding of them. We observe them often from the outside, second hand in the accounts of our patients, our loved ones and even within what our own observing egos will allow us to witness about our own traumatic experiences in our own lives.

There is no measure of reintrojection. We cannot see it, we cannot taste it, we cannot smell it. We can only notice it's consequences. We can see our patients reliving past relationships in their current lives and then we can ask them to describe it. Like stepping outside and noticing the whitened sky in long streaks after a jet has passed, we wonder what the experience of that plane ride was like. We were not on that plane, we have only been on our own trips. We could find out who was on that plane and ask them to describe that experience but we will always end up with sequential tales that come in a neat order like: "first I got my ticket, second I boarded the plane, third it took off", etc.

In the same way, we describe the process of reintrojection as if it happens one after another. The truth is, relationships with past others are being reified all of the time. The instincts of trauma victims are often so refined that they are able to know well in advance how something will play out even without going through all of the other steps in the process. The point to consider here is that reintrojection of objects is a phenomenological experience that can only be studied in its aftermath and the goal here has been to describe it's consequences and its impacts on the self and on the "others" involved.

Dissociation vs. Repression

In a relational context, dissociation becomes the primary way of repressing cognition, memory and even self-state experiences (Stern, 1993). In fact, it may be a misnomer to consider dissociation as in relationship to repression. Dissociation may be thought of as a linguistic replacement for the concept of repression. As we have seen, when we shift our thinking about the human relationships as constructed away from the idea of two people simply doing things at and to one another and into a way of thinking that implies that all human relationships are based in inter-subjective experiences involving mutual creations between the parties involved which each playing powerful and influential roles, then the relationship itself begins to define the very concept of self.

In addition, we can now think about dissociative processes as those that involve a variety of internal systems including cognitive, attentional, memory and others working in their own inter-subjective style in order to coordinate a complex defense like dissociation. Repression, on the other hand loses conceptual value when we consider what is now better understood about human information processing than it was during Freud's day. It is no longer accepted, for example that memories are stored in single locations simply waiting for us to access them like items in a phone book.

Today, we readily accept the idea that memory is first a product of attentional focus. We notice things in our environment and are constantly screening for items that require our attention. Noticing the proverbial trees in the forest is the first step in creating memory. We do not simply stack crates with slides of memories on them in some physical location in our brains. We focus our attention on a items that trigger us in one way or another and then neural pathways are created that connect thousands of existing synaptic connections that are affectively colored, informationally related and syntactically processed.

Once memories are established, they are linked to thousands of other experiences and memories. Memories then, are now less specific locations to be pinpointed and then loaded up but are more akin to processes to be joined. In this way, memories become in flux, changing constantly as a result of new neural pathways being added to existing ones in a process that is very much inter-subjective. Those new memories, now influence the way that the old ones are recalled. They are sometimes conflated, sometimes confused and sometimes even replace existing ones in our consciousness. We are all familiar with having the sensation that we are uncertain if a story that we have always "known" to be true turns out to be false when an older relative or another first hand observer hears us retell it and contradicts our details.

New models of memory formation and retrieval process shed much light on our discussion about repression vs. dissociation. As I have already suggested, repression is a term for the process whereby access to certain parts of our experience is blocked out of consciousness based on outdated notions of information processing. Once we allow ourselves to accept the idea that the notion of an engram was actually a fallacy that never really was supported with empirical evidence, we are free to accept alternative explanations for some of our defenses as well. A process-oriented understanding of memory is a natural underpinning for a process-oriented model of "forgetting" as well.

While repression may have more appeal for those of us who are challenged by the notion that if only we can untangle the factual experiences that are being repressed, as psychodynamic practitioners, researchers and theoreticians then our work will have been curative, we must however be vigilant in attempting to ensure that our theoretical models are inclusive of information being learned in neighboring disciplines; neuroscience included. We can still accept that a person is more than simply a brain stored in the confines of the body and embrace the idea that the way the brain works must be considered in our thinking about psychodynamics (Bromberg, 2003).

While better aligning with current neuroscientific literature may on it's own be reason enough to shift our thinking away from repression and toward dissociation, there are other practical considerations as well. In the preceding pages of this paper, I have attempted to make the case that enactment, projection, projective identification and the introjection of "bad" object relationships are all dissociative in nature. On one level or another, they all involve bodily systems working together to actively avoid processing of certain kinds of information that is very often initiated by an impulse to regulate affect.

For the purposes of this paper, dissociation has become a defensive process that can be considered more inclusively than can repression. By changing my thinking about what a defense actually is, I began to see dissociation as an umbrella term that better explains a whole host of defenses in a more comprehensive fashion than attempting to dissect each defense into a singular property. This paper accepts the idea that dissociative processes are at the root of most psychological defenses rather than the idea that it is simply one thing to be tackled and then moved on from.

Dissociation then moves to the center of our thinking about how psychological problems come to influence personality. We have seen that on a banal level, dissociation is simply a mentation process whereby various stimuli are attended to while others are not and are thus not committed to memory. Instead of our memory system simply running all the time like a perpetual recording device, it must be turned on in order to store information. This process is as necessary as breathing and it's no wonder that we as humans begin to do it without thinking. It is second nature. If we were not "suave" as Sullivan (1953) might have put it in regulating our stimulus responses, we would either be constantly overwhelmed or constantly in a state of paralysis, perpetually having to use conscious thought processes to wade thorough the chaff.

Perhaps as a gift of evolution we are able to discern what is safe and what is dangerous, what is food vs. what is poison and what is threat and what is comfort. Our ancestors perhaps made it off the savanna because of these natural and protective dissociative processes. One man's gift however, may turn out to be another man's trojan horse. For the trauma victim, the result of frequent vacillations of extreme overstimulation at the hands of an abuser who also serves as a needed caregiver results in a confusion of these natural dissociative processes.

What is dangerous is also what is essential, what is comforting as has the potential to become life threatening at the drop of a hat. For an infant who has no means to defend herself, this hyper-arousal process changes, in fundamental ways, how that person will utilize dissociative processes from that point forward. Pre-verbal and thus in many ways pre-symbolic, these events occur at the neural level and so, are by there very nature "unconscious" at least by the definition that we are using here in this paper.

This distortion of the natural mechanisms used by the body to regulate affect and thus control attentional focus may lie at the heart of long-term trauma reactions. As we have discussed, there is wide overlap between those who have experienced repeated trauma as a child and those who are later diagnosed with Borderline Personality Disorder. Of course, there are nature-oriented considerations like temperament that must be considered if a serious discussion of BPD is undertaken, but for our purposes, we will accept the assumption that repeated early trauma often results in symptom clusters that we have come to label (for better or for worse) Borderline Personality Disorder. This wide overlap provides a convenient way to explore the role of dissociation in victims of repeated, early childhood abuse.

In the Diagnostic and Statistical Manual (DSM IV-TR, 2000), there are 9 criteria that must be considered when one is considering making a diagnosis of BPD. Assuming that there is a reasonable amount of statistical validity and reliability, we can assume that generally speaking, these symptoms are hallmarks of trauma reactions. The criteria are:

1.   Frantic efforts to avoid real or imagined abandonment.

2.   A pattern of unstable and intense interpersonal relationships characterized by alternating between extremes of idealization and devaluation.

3.   Identity disturbance: markedly and persistently unstable self-image or   sense of self.

4.   Impulsivity in at least two areas that are potentially self-damaging (e.g.,   spending, sex, substance abuse, reckless driving, binge eating). **Note**: Do   not include suicidal or self-mutilating behavior covered in Criterion 5.

5.   Recurrent suicidal behavior, gestures, or threats, or self-mutilating   behavior

6.   Affective instability due to a marked reactivity of mood (e.g., intense   episodic dysphoria, irritability, or anxiety usually lasting a few hours   and only rarely more than a few days).

7.   Chronic feelings of emptiness

8.   Inappropriate, intense anger or difficulty controlling anger (e.g., frequent displays of temper, constant anger, recurrent physical fights)

9.   Transient, stress-related paranoid ideation or severe dissociative symptoms

While the DSM IV-TR only specifically comments on dissociation in criteria nine, it can reasonably be suggested that all of the criterion (one through nine) are all describing dissociative phenomena. Frantic efforts to avoid abandonment and a pattern of unstable relationship can be considered an inability to determine the degree to which one is securely attached in relationship or even if they can experience themselves in relationship at all as in criterion 3. Extreme impulsivity and suicidality are often unconscious acts to regulate affect which is in itself the definition of dissociation when considered from the inter-subjective perspective. Emotional lability, feelings of emptiness and extreme anger may all be reactions to dissociative processes that overwhelm the self-system in large part because one is not capable of being fully aware of what is happening to him. If, as the DSM IV-TR recommends, one needs to meet 5 of the nine criteria in order to be diagnosed with BPD, we are talking about one very dissociative individual.

Dissociation as a way of thinking about unconscious processes tied into affect relationship is a dramatically different way to think about psychodynamics. If we are constructive by nature if our personalities are indeed not static entities but are in constant movement and flux as a result of processes occurring at speed that are too fast to even be recognized, then we must consider the possibly that blocking aspects of experience from consciousness is not about "forgetting" solidified memories so much as it is about actively maintaining a process of selective attention that in many cases we have little or no conscious control over.

Trauma victims who have developed a relational style with the world that is dissociative in nature finds themselves at a disadvantage when living in a world that requires one to be able to discern what is safe and what is not. When the affect regulation system has become hard-wired to always be "on", one cannot relax. One must always be at the ready, and while hyper-vigilance is only one extreme and noticeable response to the distorting experiences that are phenomenologically lived by those who have a dissociative style, the system is in overdrive even when it cannot be seen on the outside. A near constant state of confusion leaves a person in frequent psychic distress as confusion and the condition takes its control. Dissociation truly is the cause of discontent when one cannot know for sure what is real and what is simply an artifact of a past event. This is how trauma is maintained as an everyday reality for those who suffered needlessly both as an unwitting infant and now as an adult survivor.

Affect Regulation

As a matter of course, two theoretical assumptions are central to this work. One is that a major motivating factor in the development of personality is the notion that humans are relational by nature. It is essential to their survival from the very first moments of infancy. An infant who does not learn to attach at the most primitive level is unlikely to survive much less thrive in the outside world. This acceptance of a relational model further has logical and hermeneutical expectancies that must follow and among them is that this relational tendency is elaborated throughout the body and it's various systems that are designed around the fundamental concept of survival. This includes the psychological mechanism for adjustment and the maintenance of psychological equilibrium.

The second major tenant that is at the heart of this paper is that of affect regulation. At the heart of the human relational system is a need to maintain an optimal arousal level in order to move beyond simple survival or what Sullivan termed "security operations" and toward emotionally satisfying needs. Included here is the notion of relational needs as going deeper than simply maintaing the tie in order to survive. Humans are capable of elaborate, loving relationships and as they deepen over time, greater and greater satisfaction is experienced by those within them. If a person is unable to move beyond primal affect regulation in relationship, the ability they have to deepen those relationships and move beyond security operations and into an area meaningful of mutual satisfaction.

Affect management is also at the heart of human experience. Cognitive functions (under the influence psychodynamic factors), sensory and perceptual experiences, brain functioning and neurological underpinnings work in dynamic interplay to afford us the opportunity to process the outside world and thus calm the inside world in order to enjoy our lives. Without the capacity to regulate our own affect, we would be at the mercy of the outside world, we would have no capacity to reflect on our sensations and perceptions and determine what is safe and what is not safe.

This luxury is taken for granted by most humans during most of their lives. A freak accident or even a heated argument however, can call attention to the limitations of our capacity for affect regulation. Harsh words can threaten to escalate into murderous rages and destroy relationships in the process. Leaning to consciously and unconsciously make these choices about how to respond to arousal depend heavily on the capacity for affect regulation. The self system is as essential for our survival in relationship as it was on the savanna.

For this reason, the ability of an infant to learn to self-soothe can be thought of as a major developmental milestone. While there are many factors at play that include cognitive maturation, acquisition of increasing degrees of perceived agency and even physiological considerations regarding mental capacity, the infant learning to experience a sense of safety and security in the presence of an "other" is a significant task.

If the infant is traumatized, serious threats are posed to the development of the capacity for affect regulation. For most of us, the process is unconscious. Through "good enough" mothering, the world has come to be generalized as a benevolent place. Our overarching sense is that relationships are safe vehicles for self exploration and self expression. It is a given that when we give love, we will mostly get love. While situations will arise that will require cognitive assistance to help us calm down while relating to others, this is assumed to be an exception rather than the rule. The same assumptions cannot be said for victims of trauma.

Repeated traumatic experience (particularly during infancy and early childhood) have a significant impact on the affect regulation system. Evidence is accumulating that the amygdala of traumatized individuals actually is diminished in size in comparison to those who are not traumatized. Experience influences biology in this case and traumatic experience can be as devastating to the brain as it is to the mind. Repeated trauma sets a person up to experience affective overload on a phenomenological level that appears to have physiological correlates that we are just beginning to understand.

This paper is largely concerned with the phenomenological experience of traumatized individuals and in the area of affect regulation, the experience is a challenging one. As we have seen, the capacity for affect regulation is an essential component of relational abilities for humans. In order for relationships to deepen and provide satisfaction, we must be able to experience the subjectivity of an "other" or we are bound to shift into dissociative ways of relating that are based more on internalizations of past relationships that they are on actual current experience.

One such way that this process happens relates to the self-system and the varying self-states that accompany. As we discussed earlier in this paper, self-states are experienced with memory systems, physiological correlates and affective colorations attached. When we experience a self-state that is associated with a particular memory of relating to another in a particular style, is laden with affectively-tainted emotional reactions regardless of whether or not the memory itself is a conscious thought or simply the "trace" of an experience that is felt rather than called up into explicit memory mentation.

These self-state experiences that are triggered more readily in traumatized people in part due to disturbances in the affect regulation system in the brain signal to the body that danger is present and attempts to retreat must be made. Dissociative processes take place in this phenomenological space. The self-system must regulate affect and so, it triggers a shift away from the all-too-familiar and frightening self state. By turning away from the anxiety associated with the subjective experiences of an other, a person no longer interacts directly with that other but with the representation of the other that is stored in the memory system.

Here, the potential for retraumatization is set up as the traumatized person's ability to utilize even cognitive apparatuses is diminished by his inability to accurately experience the other. And so, the projection process is triggered and he is now relating to the other as if he were someone else, someone from the past. While this experience happens on occasion to us all and we might experience something akin to de ja vu, for a traumatized person, this experience is all too common. It is dissociative in nature because it challenges one's ability to focus directly on an experience and thus commit that event to memory in the "normal" way. Instead, the experience is an amalgamation of multiple events, lacking the kind of detail that would be available to memory if the event had been the result of the mind accurately reporting the event rather than as a rapid-fire reaction based on a triggered experience.

This process is essential in the regulation of affect for victims of early childhood trauma. Affect regulation is an essential tool for all people and traumatized individuals are no exception. What is distinct is that the same tool that is utilized by non-traumatized people is now distorted. The self-system exists in all people, it is merely in overdrive for those who have had the misfortune of having the system severely disrupted at a critical period in brain development that has a major impact on what we might think of as personality development.

When we think of "hyper-vigilance" we think of it as a symptom of psychopathology that is defined by an inability to relax. This "always on" phenomenon is potentially the result of learning that relationships are not safe. The victim of repeated trauma has had their ability to relax severely impaired by the early childhood experience of needing to always be prepared for the worst. So frequent were the experiences of affect overload that the system is now hard-wired to react. Neutral affective experiences are extremely difficult to achieve. The fear of being overloaded undergirds the personality and so the capacity to relax, particularly in the presence of others is often lost.

This inability to be comfortable around others is a common experience for trauma victims. Some are hyper-sensitive and seem to find criticism in every comment. Others are in the constant startle mode whereby every off sound seems to shake them. And still others feel as if they loose part of themselves whenever they get too close to another person. This is encapsulated in the DSM IV-TR criteria 4 for Borderline Personality Disorder. Often experienced as a perceived loss of or potential loss of self, the trauma victim behaves as if he is about to be destroyed at any moment by some great threat that feels to them as if it is present in nearly every situation; often even when they are sleeping.

One can imagine from this point of view, the tremendous challenges associated with having a flawed affect regulation system. While organic and brain-oriented underpinnings help to provide empirical support for a phenomenological experience that is such a threat to so many, in some ways it lacks the descriptive power to help us to understand what the experience of having a dissociative style is all about. As we have said, even looking at the engine of a jet plane provides little understanding for what it feels like to fly in one.

Psychodynamically speaking, the victim of repeated trauma experiences a tension in relationships. He is unable to comfortably settle into the mutual vulnerability that is so important to the development of deepening relationships. His internalized object representations are defined by intense anxiety to the point of overload. The objective experience of a subjective other is nearly precluded entirely. A boss, a lover and even a close friend will likely become assimilated to the stored memory of the terrorizing other and thus stimulate a stunning emotional shock.

With this in mind, it is easy to comprehend how relationships are often experienced as unstable by traumatized individuals. In the common language of our time, we use language like "he's damaged goods" and say that they are "playing head games" in part because we have such an immense difficulty understanding what it is like to forge new relationships when we have a head full of nothing but bad memories of relationships.

The self-system and it's affect regulation system are a key component of what makes dissociation such a central component of maintaining trauma as an everyday life experience in the life of a traumatized individual. If one cannot stay comfortably within a single self-state and are constantly being lashed about, one is unlikely to be able to tolerate the uncertainty of an "other" who has the potential to hurt them. As one moves from self-state to self-state, one loses vital information that has the capacity to change their perception of events and thus keep them from being retraumatized.

Modern imaging technique has enabled us to actually identify key brain areas that likely underlie psychodynamic phenomenon. When combined with language that provides the due sensitivity to the human experience, we now can use this empirical evidence to promote greater understanding among clinicians who complain about "difficult clients" and among the general public who interact with victims of repeated trauma and are bewildered by their behavior. This is a hope of this paper. By promoting understanding, we promote compassion and by promoting compassion, we promote healing.

Clinical Implications

As this work continues to explore the experiences of those who have been "traumatized", it is important that we consider the implications of what we have described in earlier sections of this work. One of the most insidious repercussions of the traumatic experience is that is does not end once physical safety has been secured. As is all too painfully known, simply removing an abused child from an abusive home environment is not enough to undo all of the damage that can be done by a caregiver.

For those who have had the misfortune of repeated trauma being a feature of their intra-psychic developmental experience, the stage is set for a re-enactment of those early childhood experiences as he attempts to remain connected to the essential-but-abusive caregivers upon which their identity is based. As we have noted, the abused child does not separate from their caregivers in the same way that those who have not been traumatized do. Their individuation is thwarted and the child's psyche splits, leaving him attached to the painful internalized object representations that allow him to feel as though he is still alive.

This attachment to object representations that are both essential and threatening and essential forms the basis for the dissociative processes that define this work. An abused child (who may even be preverbal) cannot rectify the split dichotomy that exists between the good and needed caregiver and the frightening and traumatizing abuser. And so, he splits, quarantining areas of her psychic experience from one another, limiting access to conscious experience and the self-states that are attached to those fully divided experiences of the "others" involved and even themselves.

When victims of repeated trauma finally come to a therapist for help, it generally is quite often due to problematic relationships that seem to be the source of more pain than pleasure. The prospect of connecting to others is dangerous and incredibly triggering for someone who's sense of self is based largely on traumatic interactions with frightening others. Each new relationship has the potential to trigger her to unconsciously access previously dissociated material and the self-states attached to them. Over and over, traumatized individuals find new relationships that first appeared to be exciting and genuine opportunities for healing to eventually cloud over and become stressful as they feel long-warded off pain and anxiety.

Further, through processes like projection, projective identification and re-introjection, these new relationships come to resemble old ones as the internal world is now projected into the outside world. This re-enactment process has often come to define the relationships of those we have come to know as traumatized, and as clinicians, we must be aware that these tendencies to maintain ties to old object representations and relational patterns will also come through the door with our patients.

Within the affect-regulation model of personality structure and development, it is essential that we realize that our presence, as hopeful as it may be, will also be a tremendously stimulating experience for a traumatized person. That stimulation will very likely trigger a need for affect-regulation which is at the heart of why they are seeking treatment in the first place. Regardless of a therapist's theoretical orientation or primary treatment modality, the patient will bring to the work their own histories and relational patterns. Preparing for this potential is essential and must be a consideration when any traumatized person is brought into any treatment paradigm.

The question that is posed here then becomes a challenge to the clinician. How do we engage in a relationship with these souls who desperately need our help without becoming drawn into the pattern, leaving us unable to help? Worse still, our potential to contribute to the re-introjection process makes us an even greater potential threat.

As authority figures who are sought out for help with emotional struggle, there is enormous potential to be of help to those who are struggling under the enormous weight of past trauma. Men and women engage in therapy because they believe that help is possible and they quietly watch us for signs that we will be able to soothe their pain and help them find a way to navigate through their pain and establish a new way of relating to others.

In addition to our potential to heal, we also have the potential to make things worse. Accessing an authority figure that is fantasized to be something of a parental figure to a traumatized individual is incredibly triggering and that must be taken into consideration as we approach traumatized individuals. Before they enter the consultation room, it is often the case that the patient will have fantasized enormous hopes and fears into the relationship and we will scarcely be aware of it.

In his work The Iatrogenics Handbook: A Critical Look at Research & Practice in Helping Professions (Twemlow, S.W. and Gabbard, G.O., 2004), the authors asks us to consider the unconscious dialogue between clinician and patient that may contribute to the patients therapeutic process in a dilitarious fashion. Describing the process as an "unconscious collusion between doctor and patient resulting in a matrix of miscommunication" (109), he asks us to be ever wary of the potential (and even insidious) collaboration between the two parties that may be unconscious and thus out of awareness. While our intents are most certainly good (or at least benign) we must attempt to bring our best attempts to understand our own wishes and desires to consciousness as often as we attempt to do with those of our patients. Full awareness is never possible but an ethical approach to practice with our patients (victims of trauma or otherwise) involves a commitment to the perpetual development of greater self awareness.

In addition, we are surely not a blank slate. Each of us who have taken up the mantle of responsibility of becoming considered "healers" by our culture brings with us our own history of abuse and of traumatizing relational interactions that have left us with our own frightening internalized object representations to which we cling for the maintenance of our own attachments and identities. Without awareness of this layer of the therapeutic encounter, we are quite likely to do as much harm as good.

Psychodynamic case formulation and assessment are an essential component of work with traumatized individuals. We must learn to become as aware of our own counter-transference and susceptibility to projective identification as is humanly possible. If we inadvertently slip into the patients relational patterns we have not only joined the re-introjection process, we have now had a potential impact on the person's potential for healing in the future.

The tendency to split and generalize experience is a hallmark of trauma and it is easy for this new therapist to come to represent all therapists. As clinicians, we are familiar with patients who come to therapy with sad histories of past therapists who were not mindful of their own potential to engage in a non-therapeutic style of relating to the patient. The result (due to the re-introjection process) is often greater resistance to full engagement, a cognitive barrier to accepting us as healing and even an increase in the use of defense in order to protect themselves from our potential threat.

What then, is to be done about this conundrum? While this paper is not a clinical manual and the expertise of this author is limited due to relative inexperience, there are some clinical implications to be considered generally that will likely establish a greater potential for success in the clinical encounter than for failure.

Carl Rogers is most known for his belief in the intrinsic capacity for people to heal themselves from emotional trauma (Rogers,1995). His belief in this propensity for reparation underlies all of his theoretical writings. With this in mind, Rogers suggested that our role as clinicians is to provide the necessary conditions for a positive therapeutic outcome. Coining the phrase "unconditional positive regard", Rogers held fast to the belief that we must first accept our clients where they are and believe in their innate capacity to seek out healing if we are to be of help.

Without an attitude of unconditional positive regard, we run the risk of judging our patients. When we judge our patients, we run the risk of re-traumatizing them without conscious awareness. Traumatized individuals are innately sensitive to subtle shifts in relational dialogue. They had to be. During critical periods in development, they were forced to be come finely attuned to their caregiver's mood states, attitudes and behaviors toward them. Their survival was dependent upon it. We must then choose to identify and accept the maneuvers that our patients employ in order to avoid triggering and re-traumatizing them.

Triggering of internalized object representations is inevitable in the clinical process just as it is in all relationships for traumatized individuals. In fact, it is a necessary component of their treatment. If we accept that re-enactment is a part of the healing process, then we must be ever-conscious of the process rather than as passive participants who contribute to completing the cycle without knowing it. While it may seem like a contradiction to suggest that we must avoid triggering our traumatized patients while at the same time using the reaction to a triggering as part of the therapeutic interaction, a closer look reveals that it is actually quite intuitive.

Our role as therapists is to challenge the cycle and seek out new potential for the emergence of new relational possibilities. We must notice when our patient's have been triggered into new self-states and therefore access to dissociated material. Without this experiential component, our ability to provide healing is extremely limited. It is well established in psychoanalytic literature that insight alone is not sufficient to provide healing. Intellectual inquiry and understanding are of help to the patient to be sure but we must be ever wary that insight alone is unlikely to change core components of the person's pattern-oriented method of interacting with "others". We must go deeper and work within an actual experience rather than an abstraction.

While many clinicians are naturally uncomfortable with this suggestion due to our own anxieties about accessing sensitive material and the potential to contribute to the re-traumatization process, that is not reason enough to neglect our role. Trauma patients are injured in relationship to others and so the healing must also too occur within relationship. If we know that relating to others is what triggers the dissociative process, we must be aware that it will happen in our encounters with traumatized individuals and we must learn to use it.

Specific to Roger's notion of unconditional positive regard, we must promote our own understanding of the essential (if temporary) prophylactic nature of these defense mechanisms. They were developed as a means to stay attached to needed others and to the selves. The enactments that will inevitably be resistant to treatment are part of a process (that while flawed) has served an important function in helping traumatized individuals continue to experience themselves as whole. With this in mind, we must remember what it is that we are asking them to do.

Without much risk of overstating the point, it is my contention that when we ask a traumatized person to give up their defensive attachment to their internalized object relations and the self-states that accompany them, we are asking them to risk everything. Without those attachments there is tremendous fear that there will be no comfort, no soothing, and potentially, no self. By maintaining a formal stance for our clients and their defenses, we stand a better chance that they will agree to slowly relinquish those attachments and begin to live in the shared world of subjective others.

As I have stated earlier in this writing, this is not a clinical manual and specific treatment recommendations are being purposefully avoided and I will continue to maintain that stance. With that in mind, it is also a consideration of this paper that the enactment processes in inevitable and essential. When our patients are in an enactment process, they now have much more access to the dissociated material and the self-states attached to them and therefore an immense opportunity to be of help is afforded.

While we may be uncomfortable with the material that is being accessed, the self-states that we are witnessing or even be reaching the point of our own affective overload, we must remember that without the actual experience being brought into the room, there is little hope that we will be of much help in the process (Davies and Frawley, 1991). Within the enactment process (when experienced within the relative safety of the therapeutic alliance), the person has the opportunity to expand their conscious awareness of the previously dissociated material and phenomena and this potential cannot be overstated even though it can be ignored.

This therapeutic enactment process carries with it all of the due respect and carefulness we expect it would. We are entrusted with the awareness of the process that we are to help our patients bring out of the darkness and into the light. We must maintain our stance of unconditional positive regard in order to communicate to them in ways that will encourage a further deepening of their experience rather than triggering them to avoid the experience when they sense our judgment or discomfort.

With this in mind, we must be careful not to interpret too quickly. If we jump the gun due to our own inability to handle the material that is being newly accessed, we risk teaching the patient that what they already fear is intolerable, is indeed intolerable. Our traumatized patients have learned hypervigilance as a way of maintaining their safety as well as their own. Avoiding the existential dread that so often accompanies the warded-off material was a well-learned and much-needed skill and we must avoid strengthening that tendency to escape rather than learn to experience.

As we have noted, there are many limitations to what we are capable of as clinicians. It is particularly noteworthy to recognize the physiological correlates to the psychodynamic interplay that we are describing. Our developing brains are impacted by the relational experiences that happen during our infancy and childhood. In fact, they define them. We must be cautious to note that our patients healing will not strictly depend upon their ability to think their way out of these long-standing relational patterns.

If our client's ability to regulate his serotonin levels is impacted by developmental processes, he will struggle with affect regulation. If our patient's hippocampus has had its growth complicated by stimulus overload, he will have memory difficulties. And, if our client has anomalies with his Brocca's area as a result of childhood trauma, he will have difficulty finding words to express his feelings, memories and symbolizing his experiences. These challenges are of course, not imminently visible but they are no less important. To deny them in favor of easy explanations and treatment manuals does not serve our clients or our practices well.

Our ability to heal as clinicians is limited. We are not miracle workers who can magically alleviate the pain and suffering that our patients have spent their lifetimes living with. We cannot erase all of the internalized object relationships, we cannot comfort every self-state that they trigger and most of all, we cannot erase the fact that our patients have been abused, beaten and terrorized in unimaginable ways.

What we can do is help our clients learn to tolerate their own experience. If we can stay with them and refuse to dissociate ourselves away from the frightening material like our patients are prone to do, new hope is established. Very often, our patients are cognitively and unconsciously looking to us to tell them if what they fear is as scary as they believe it is. We must learn to tolerate their pain if they are to learn to do the same.

If we rush to interpret, we not only have closed off certain healing avenues, we have also unconsciously reified their belief that the material is shameful and should be avoided. And, because so much of our patient's identity is attached to that material, we are also subtly suggesting that they themselves are shameful as well.

As therapists, we can be of help to those who are suffering. We can offer them a model of a new way of relating to others. We can also demonstrate to them that their material will not destroy us or them if it is allowed conscious access. These are tremendous gifts that we can offer our patients and they are gifts that they have been waiting for for a very long time. If we can learn to accept our own intolerable material, then perhaps they can learn to do so as well.

Breaking the stalemate of dissociative processes that leave our clients returning to the same relational patterns over and over again is a challenge that is endeavored collaboratively between patient and therapist. There are no guarantees and there is potential to do harm. Our responsibility to learn our own triggers, our own dissociative processes and to learn to tolerate them is at the heart of learning to be successful in treating traumatized individuals. Perhaps the potential to be of help can provide us with the impetus to learn more about ourselves and about the experiences of our patients.

Conclusion to the Discussion

In large part, this paper begins with inter-subjective and affect-regulation based understanding of the development of personality. If we consider the human personality as forming within the context of relationship to the outside world, we begin to think about the tremendous impact that the early infant relationships must necessarily play in the developing mind of a young child. A young child who is treated well in the comforting and nourishing arms of a loving mother develops a sense of safety, recognizes his own and others' potential for destruction but learns to integrate and sublimate that sensed possibility and ultimately develops a sense that the world is a supportive place where he can learn to live, love and grow with the expectation that safety and security are more or less assumed.

If a child does not manage to be fortunate enough to be reared in a loving and nurturing environment, the potential for relational templates to be established in infancy that will last throughout the lifespan are greatly increased. Trauma and its sequela are incredibly impacting events that do not cease to influence the person once the trauma has ended. The consequences of early life abuse are long-lasting and can, in some instances, come to define the operational style of its victims. It spoils one's development of relational templates and creates a frightening inter-subjective field that is incredibly frightening place for a young child. In addition, one of infancies great developmental challenges (to learn to develop affect regulation abilities) is impacted on both psychodynamic and on physiological levels.

If we accept that regulating affect within a person's relational field is a major component of the development of a more or less stable presentational style, otherwise known as personality, than we must consider the impact that early life experience within that field has on children. This work embraces the notion that trauma (particularly when perpetrated) by needed caregivers creates psychological challenges in the area of affect regulation and inter-subjective experience as key components of psychopathology. It is also accepted that traumatic insults that do leave these frustrating imprints in style contribute to the overall operating style of traumatized individuals that can prevent tragic experiences from remaining remnants of a frightening but distant past, but keeps them as recurring experiences that contribute to a cycle of retraumatization. With this in mind, the Object Relations theorists inform this paper greatly from a psychoanalytic understanding of human personality development.

The Object Relations perspective on enactment is one key component of the retraumatization cycle as described in this paper. Enactment is the process whereby traumatized individuals attempt to maintain ties to past perpetrators who very often served the dual role of being necessary caregivers. This confusing relationship sets up a trauma victim to necessitate a replication process whereby he is able to maintain contact with these needed caregivers as well as himself.

From the Object Relations perspective, negative object interactions are introjected and thus form the template for future interactions with others. Introjected object representations are not pleasant memories of joyous and nurturing interactions with loved ones. They are memory traces of frightening interactions that lead very often to affect overload, terror, the fear of annihilation and even physical insult. They are the stuff of nightmares lived in the light of day on an unconscious level.

The trauma victim comes to experience the world and the "others" in it as frightening and thus, something to be retreated from. Turning inward, the traumatized person shifts her energetic and libidinal possibility inward and away from growth toward the outside world. Describing this process as ultimately anti-libidinal is for all practical purposes, an understatement. The development of dissociation away from the outside world as a defense against experience repeated so often in the real world (that they are now existential fears of annihilation and self dissolution) is a far more destructive event than the term implies.

To suggest that something is anti-libidinal is merely to say that something does not promote life. The creation and maintenance of internalized object representations goes much further. It not only inhibits development in psychological growth, it actively promotes retreat. One who dissociates is frozen in time, unable to use the world and it's others who inhabit it as springboards to movement, they are like magnets, forever pushing the person away.

In the enactment process, the person is able to be triggered into self-state experiences that are affectively colored and familiar. In the enactment process, one is once again close to the others who she once needed but also abused her. She is also closer to herself because her personality development was, at a critical time, dependent on being in reaction to frightening others.

While enactment may help one maintain her needed ties to past caregivers and even act as proof of her own existence, it has its costs in the form of affective overload which triggers the self system to begin further dissociative processes that cause the trauma victim to miss pertinent information. Included in that information is that the new person who is part of the enactment is not the same as the internalized object representation and that the world is no longer a frightening place -- that peace is possible.

Within this process of enactment, the defensive process of projection also plays a key role. The highly traumatized person is dissociative in nature. As a child, he learned to separate experiences from one another, to freeze and even to generate self trance in order to maintain physical safety, to separate himself from the caregivers who might destroy and contrastingly, to find psychological space whereby he may maintain needed ties to those caregivers and his own sense of self.

These dissociative processes contribute to relational patterns that are likely to continue to impact his method of creating and maintaining relationships into his adult life. Projection is essential to that person because it allows the enactment process to function. In projection, the trauma victim is first triggered to re-experience self-states that are dissociated from consciousness. Without awareness, he has experienced a powerful reminder of his early life experience.

Once the person is triggered, he is now set up to begin to project those early life relationship templates onto the person with whom he is now relating. Without awareness, attributes that are unconsciously identified are projected onto the new person and in essence, he is the perpetrator from so long ago. Along with that projection comes all of the fear, anxiety and other unwanted material that has been dissociated away from the conscious ego. The projector rarely knows that that the projection process is in place. So powerful is this dissociative tendency that he has little or no awareness that he has been triggered or that he is now acting on that trigger as if the internalized object representation were actually present in the interaction that he is now experiencing.

Once the person has begun to project his relational templates onto the outside world, the potential for a projective identification process to be initiated has become magnified. In projective identification, the frightening material associated with the internalized object representations now needs someplace to go. The trauma victim must find a way to discharge this material that is both dissociated and ultimately frightening. He cannot contain that frightening material and so it must be externalized. Just as in projection internal material is projected outward into the interpsychic world, so too does projective identification get cast off the trauma victim and onto others. In this case, it is projected into others.

In projective identification, the frightening and unbearable material cannot be tolerated within the individual just as it had not been tolerable as an infant. A frightened child without the developmental capacity to process terror, anxiety and fears of annihilation must get rid of the material and so it is projected into the caregiver who can handle the material and also can begin to react to it. In a safe environment, the mother is responsive and soothes the child, providing the necessary sustenance and comfort. In a traumatizing environment, the mother is unable or unwilling to provide that response and so she reacts to the material now inside her with her own fears and anxieties. Potentially, she retaliates.

Like the child, the adult who projects his unwanted material into others must now deal with the consequences of dealing with an "other" who will have his own reaction to the material. That reaction may, like the frightening caregiver, retaliate, may draw closer or may reject the victim. Each of these potential reactions is based on the individual receiving the material's own experience with internalized object representations, but each will have an impact that is potentially retraumatizing to one or both parties involved. All occurring unconsciously through dissociative processes, both parties may be unsuspecting of what will befall them.

From this vantage point, it is much easier to see how projective identification can contribute to a retraumatization process. Once one has projected her unwanted material into an other, he no longer can control the outcome. If he is rejected, he may re-experience the traumatic rejection that was heaped upon him by a neglectful mother who was unable to bond with him due to her inability to get beyond her own needs or potentially due to her own experience with trauma. If he retaliates, he is likely to subject the trauma victim to new trauma that reintrojects the old objects who retaliated against their own guilt, shame, anxiety or fear of annihilation. Finally, if he joins him in the cycle by pulling closer, the potential for the two to work in tandem to perpetuate the cycle is immense.

Like soul mates, two trauma victims may find each other and fit together like lock and key. Creating a rapid cycling back and forth between them that leaves each of them projecting and becoming receptors of one another's unwanted anxieties in reciprocal projective identification processes. Perhaps the "joining and drawing close" reaction is the most frightening because the potential for emotional, physical and sexual violence is so great. The interlocking defensive styles can be immensely triggering and can leave both open to new wounds atop the old ones that generated the cycle to begin with.

The retraumatization cycle as proposed by Davies and Frawley (1991) and explored in this paper is fueled by dissociative processes at every turn. Trauma and it's sequela overwhelm the system and circumvent natural libidinal processes in favor of anti-libidinal and growth inhibiting, destructive ones. The consequences are life-long as physiological correlates seem to undergird these processes virtually guaranteeing that they will continue.

Child abuse and neglect are quite possibly the number one public health concern that we face as a nation. Statistics suggest that we spend more money on the consequences of child abuse than we do on several of the disease-killers of our day. The untold emotional consequences contribute to crime, domestic violence and existential unrest in otherwise civilized societies. It is the hope of this paper to understand the process of dissociation as a reaction to trauma on the human psyche and personality and to promote greater understanding of these processes in the clinical community and in the world at large.

CHAPTER V. CONCLUSION

The main goal of this work was to explore the role that dissociation plays in a re-traumatization cycle proposed by Davies and Frawley (1991). In the process of studying the phenomenon, it became clear that several logical and hermeneutic hurdles first had to be overcome. In fact, as the study continued, understanding personality development and the relating patterns of people in general became essential components of understanding the process by which one is traumatized in the first place.

A significant premise of this work hinges on the assumption that underlying personality development is first a libidinal drive within the human being and that drive a is drive to connect to the outside world in general and to the "others" in it in particular. The very survival of a human is dependent on his ability to connect to the other humans with whom he shares the world and that need to connect is fraught with potential for failure.

Within the mother-infant dyad is an essential learning process that informs both personality development and underlying physiological correlates. A successful relational environment that is built and maintained by successful caregivers sets the stage for a human personality that has several advantages when setting off into the outside world. He has learned that the world is relatively benign and he has learned that he has the skills and abilities needed to succeed in it.

The unsuccessful dyad however, leaves the infant fearful of the world and with the feeling that he lacks what it takes to succeed. This early life experience has both the unfortunate developmental impact on the child that valuable brain functioning is impacted that will limit memory and language making abilities and will affect the object relations system that helps the infant maintain a sense of connection to himself and to others in the world.

Trauma creates fragmentation as described by Judith Herman (1992), a bad self as is experienced when one is attempting to comprehend one's abuse cannot be reconciled with a good self and so they cannot integrate. A failure of depressive rapprochement contributes to a failure of reconciliation within psyche, and so the splitting continues. The self has not fully developed in this way. It is forever burdened with the anxiety associated with annihilation that is experienced by frightened infants. It has not shifted into an integration of its ability to survive on its own. The messages received were far too frightening to be successfully processed.

When the infant is traumatized, he is unable to manage the affect experienced and so he learns to dissociate between self-states in order to seek out safe refuge within his personality. This habit becomes so engrained that the infant grows up dissociating as standard procedure whenever he is threatened with affect that he unconscious believes he is unable to withstand. This tendency places the growing personality at a tremendous advantage.

Dissociating (while packing immediate prophylactic effects) has its discontents. When dissociative processes come to define one's operational style, one misses valuable information. That key information is what makes a person able to notice that the world has changed; that he is no longer in danger and that he can now form relationships that will not threaten his sense of self. Without that information, the person is left with only internalized object representations rather than with the actual other "subjects" that share the world with him.

While dissociating when triggered by external cues by the environment and by others in the world, the object representations that were once so needed for survival now contribute to their own re-introjection and to the re-traumatization cycle. The adult victim of trauma did not develop a sense of self as separate from his abuser. His need for survival depended upon maintaining attachment to his caregivers and to becoming attuned to their every shift. A missed cue may have resulted in a beating and a return of the anxiety associated with a fear of death.

Now an adult, the trauma victim must maintain a tie to those introjected objects and to his sense of self. As a result, he must project those internalized feelings onto others around him who quite often will react to the fearful material in ways that contribute to his re-traumatization. He may react with anger due to his own introjections or he may reject. Either way, the result is more pain and suffering experienced by the already reeling trauma victim.

This constant shifting between self-states was once the hallmark of the self-systems attempt to soothe the self when it was unable to do so using other means. As an adult, the process continues to be an affect-modulation tool but it now prevents a traumatized person from learning other methods. In addition, it prevents the trauma victim from recognizing the others in his life as distinct from the abusers who once frightened him so badly. In the mind of the trauma victim, subjective others are frightening and so they are avoided due to the fear of being overloaded and ultimately destroyed.

As we have seen in this study, memory and the unconscious along with it are continually created. There is no great storage closet where bad memories are packaged up and locked away. Memories, sensations, perceptions and experiences are continually recreated as new events occur. Old events influence the perception of new ones and new ones change the perceptions of old ones.

This process lends itself to dissociation as a process that ultimately serves the person in his ability to attune to necessary experience and ignore banal ones is now usurped by a process that prevents a person from conscious attentional focus and thus new learning. Dissociation is far more common and everyday than was once thought and considered alongside modern empirical data, appears to be a more accurate description of processes that keep traumatized people from recalling information, memories and experiences from their past and that keep them in a recurrent trauma cycle.

Dissociation is withdrawal, denial of the actual world in favor of an internal world where perceived locus of control is greater. This may serve the infant well in the short-term but the long-term consequences are devastating. We have learned that a dissociative style of dealing with the outside world leaves a traumatized adult at a major disadvantage in relating to the outside world. In many ways, he has not learned to relate with actual subjective others and so is left to live with the demons of his introjected past.

In many ways, this paper has explored the fundamental questions posed at the outset of the study. The chief goal of this paper was exploration, and in that sense, the results are significant. While there are many unanswered questions about the role of dissociation in a re-traumatization cycle, some better understanding has been achieved and some new questions for future study have been discovered. In the future, it is hoped that some of these questions will also have their day of study by this author and others who seek to provide relief to those who suffer throughout their lives due to the emotional injuries experienced so early on.

Early childhood trauma victims have been forced to endure experiences that are unspeakable to most of us. They have learned methods of coping with emotional overload that at one time allowed them to survive and even thrive in the face of torment. By attempting this inquiry it has been my hope to give voice to the voiceless and to provide understanding for those who do not have words to ask for that understanding on their own.

Limitations

This goal of this study has been to better understand the role of dissociation in a re-traumatization cycle that maintains trauma as a going concern for individuals who have suffered repeated trauma during the early years of their life. It is my hope that this paper has shed some light on the unconscious processes that maintain this cycle in order to be of help to those who are suffering.

This work has endeavored to be as rigorous as possible in maintaining a scholarly attitude toward the existing research as well as when attempting to extrapolate beyond that work and into new theoretical territory. I have also attempted to put aside biases about what might be happening in order to focus first on the research questions and seeking out answers for those questions.

In many respects, this work has failed in its ability to be completely unbiased. As a clinician and as a person who has spent time observing others in relationship, the course of time has led me to draw several conclusions based on anecdotal evidence and based on my own experience. While intuition is not wholly inappropriate as a methodological approach to "knowing" something to be true, it can also cloud one's judgment and limit access to objectivity.

With this in mind, this paper maintains a stance of being more descriptive than prescriptive. It has been my attempt to use psychoanalytic language to describe processes that are not observable with microscopes or even measurable with even the most sophisticated technology. In addition, with the exception of the neuropsychological literature, I have opted to avoid quantitative evidence in favor of utilizing logic and hermeneutic methodology as evidence to support claims made within this work. This will inevitably lead to criticism that this paper is unavailable for replication.

The processes described in this paper do not lend themselves to observation very easily. In fact, one cannot actually see dissociation and so one is left to take note of the consequences of these processes that we believe to exist and then to describe what is likely to have transpired. With that in mind, this paper has attempted to faithfully describe these processes based on the evidence found in the existing literature and in my own case material.

This work also can also make no claim that processes involved are more prevalent in traumatized than non-traumatized persons. While we cite rates of BPD and other trauma-related disorders, we cannot state that we have found rates of dissociation to be greater among participants in this study over the general population. We can notice patterns, cite existing literature, and use the voices of our clients to suggest and describe but we cannot prove.

In response to potential criticism of the methodology presented in this literature I can only offer that I have attempted to be rigorous and faithful to the evidence that I have selected for use in this book. This study is not replicable and I make no claim that it should be. It should be considered against other evidence and then the portions that continue to make sense and provide useful descriptive evidence of psychodynamic phenomena should continue to be explored. The rest should be discarded as better evidence is gathered.

This work has attempted to faithfully collate several different types of literature from several fields in order to promote greater understanding within a particular linguistic framework. It is of course entirely possible that other disciplines can provide equal or even better insight and understanding of the phenomena presented in this work. It is accepted by this author that there are multiple ways of knowing and each has much to add to this body of evidence.

To understand the value of this work and others like it, one must accept that there are phenomena that do not lend themselves to quantitative evaluation. By creating a rich description of the experiences of those entrusted to the care of psychodynamic-oriented clinicians like myself I hope to move beyond prevalence rates and behavioral observations and into areas that consider the multiple dimensions of human life with those of traumatized persons being of particular interest to this study.

While quantitative evidence is enormously helpful in helping us understand clinical phenomenon, it too has limitations. It is, for example, less helpful when it comes to helping clinicians understand the experiential component that our patients will describe. In this way, qualitative and theoretical work can help us to deepen our empathic understanding of what is happening on the inside of the patient's world rather than simply standing at the edge and looking for behavioral observations.

This work has placed an enormous value on the individual experience of patients who have been traumatized. It has been my attempt to utilize language that has been helpful in expanding my own interpretation of patients/ experiences so that my ability to communicate understanding, respect and appreciation for their attempts at regulating their affective worlds.

This language, born out of psychoanalytic experience beginning with Freud's observations and continuing through the writings of contemporary scholars like Jessica Benjamin (1990) and Davies & Frawley (1999), continue to have much to offer the field of psychology and I hope to have contributed in some small way to the respect for continuation of this way of conceptualizing human behavior that leaves room for behavior and the interpretation of that behavior.

Finally, a significant limitation of this study is the inability to fully integrate the quantitative evidence provided by neuropsychology and cognitive science. There are both political and natural limitations to that integration. Some in the field find little use in assimilating the work. For those of us who do see value in identifying physiological correlates to psychoanalytic phenomena, we often find a dearth of existing literature that has carved out a way to utilize the terminology employed by each in ways that are comprehensible to both fields. I found this an enormous challenge in both the research and synthesis phases of this work.

Taken together, it is my hope that this work is recognized for its desire to promote better understanding of the human condition in general and in the defensive patterns employed in the affect regulation process of traumatized individuals in general. In spite of its obvious (and not so obvious) limitations, it has been incredibly rewarding to dig deeply into the existing literature and identify common themes and elements that provide the foundation of this paper. In this regard, I am extremely grateful to have had the opportunity.

Future Research

While many of the areas that I consider important elements of future research are covered in the area of this paper relating to the clinical implications of this study, there are several key elements that lend themselves to study that are neither addressed in this study nor well distributed in existing literature. From the point of view of this author, this study is exploratory in nature and therefore belongs at the beginning of the research cycle. Key ideas presented here have little quantitative support and are much deserving of further study.

As I have stated in this study, I believe that dissociation is a key component of the process whereby traumatization is a recurrent theme in the lives of the victims of early childhood trauma and for that reason, I hope that greater emphasis will be placed on exploration of those implications in future theoretical, phenomenological and quantitative research.

One area that I believe deserves much attention is in identifying dissociative processes in a laboratory setting. While this is an enormous challenge that likely surpasses our current imaging techniques, if we can support the hypothesis that dissociation is not only a common experience for victims of trauma but also a major feature in the maintenance of it, then we can ask the culture at large to accept this phenomena and draw their attention to it. In an age where image is such a potent attention-grabber, our ability to demonstrate psychological phenomenon using modern imaging techniques will serve the fields of psychology in general and psychoanalysis in general quite well.

Another area of future research applies to clinical practice. By promoting greater awareness of dissociative phenomenon, it is my hope that better training procedures can be established to help clinicians recognize these events. By helping clinicians notice when their patients are slipping into dissociative processes, we can help them to interrupt the trauma cycle. In fact, helping clinicians recognize dissociation will likely have the effect of helping patients recognize them as well. Clinical research on multiple levels will help develop the assessment skills employed by the clinical community and promote general awareness of the phenomenon.

In addition to helping clinicians recognize dissociation, future research might develop effective treatment strategies to help patients learn to recognize their own dissociative patterns as well as tolerate the anxiety that trigger them. Developing treatment recommendations helps patients and their therapists learn to work collaboratively in the process of understanding the particular ways and times that dissociation occurs for each unique patient will go a long way toward interrupting the cycle of retraumatization as proposed here.

With this in mind, I have come to consider my own clinical work and to suggest that the practice of mindfulness may help to expand the awareness of dissociative trends in our patient's experience. Much research exists that suggest that bodily and sensory awareness by patients has a positive treatment effect on Borderline Personality Disorder and this may be due to an interruption of the dissociative process (Linehan, Armstrong, Suare, Allmon and Heard, 1991).

It is also fairly well established that mindfulness has the positive effect of reducing anxiety levels of patients who struggle with it as a way of life (Fletcher and Kabat-Zinn, 1995). If we assume that the affect associated with anxiety is analogous to the intra-psychic and unconscious anxiety that is being warded off through dissociative processes, than it is fair to assume that mindfulness can be utilized to help patients discover and tolerate and safely explore that anxiety as part of psychodynamic treatment.

I also hope that further research could help develop mindfulness routines that would enable our patients to expand their conscious awareness of psychological phenomenon and promote the tolerance of that phenomena through interventions designed to promote acceptance and knowledge of the experience.

Finally, this paper accepts that dissociation is but one component of the retraumatization process and each phase in this process, if explored, is likely to expand our awareness of the cycle. Through quantitative, hermeneutic and qualitative study, I hope that this cycle will continue to be explored and that the evidence collected will be presented to the clinicians and to the general public. In this way, we can continue to reduce the terrible burden that childhood trauma places on our society and on the individuals who have experienced it.

Final Thoughts

This work was initiated as an attempt to help the author understand a retraumatization cycle as proposed by Davies and Frawley (1991). By examining the literature found in several different bodies of literature, I have learned much about the process in general and about dissociation in particular. The work has been a tremendous challenge full of confirmation and also full of contradiction.

The human mind is an incredibly complex blend of systems and processes that work in a comprehensive fashion to help the human survive both physically and psychologically. In fact, as I looked closer and closer at these phenomena, one thing in particular came into exquisite focus along the way. The human being is an incredibly unique and adaptive creature that has an incredible capacity to develop methods for survival.

I have learned about the human capacity to love and to connect with one another and I have learned that it is precisely that ability to do so, despite tremendous odds, that gives life to the human personality. Early family experiences have the power to create incredible resiliency and even among the most traumatized, the human spirit and libidinal drive toward a fulfilling life cannot be fully extinguished.

In fact I have come to believe the enactment process itself, is an incredibly powerful example of the human ability to heal itself. As a traumatized soul continues to reenter relationship with others in spite of all of the fear and anxiety that his early life instilled in him, he does so with a desire to heal. Within the metaphor of the enactment process are all of the inspiring elements that make humans such a fascinating species to behold. Our lives are destined to have meaning and our relationships help us make that meaning. It is as if the human soul recognizes that the potential to connect to deeper things in life lies in relationship to others and so we try again and again in order to find that meaning.

Childhood trauma is a dangerous phenomena that has an impact on the young lives that are directly impacted by the severe abuse and neglect that is so often the initiator of so much pain in life. By continuing to explore the self-healing processes (while potentially re-traumatizing) triggered by the initial trauma, we are both educating the public about the danger of child abuse and learning to help those who are most in need of it. I hope that this paper continues to be one

of many to explore the avenues of understanding and

eventual healing for those who wait for answers to their

suffering.

REFERENCES

Bailey, John (Producer), Ramis, Harold (Director). (1993). *Groundhog Day*[Theater].

Benjamin, J. (1990). Recognition and Destruction: An Outline of Intersubjectivity. *Psychoanalytic Psychology*, *7*, 33-47. In S. A. Mitchell & L. Aron (Eds.), *Relational Psychoanalysis: the Emergence of a Tradition*. Hillsdale, NJ: Analytic Press.

Broadbent, D. E. (1958). *Perception and communication*. New York, NY: Pergamon Press.

Bromberg, P. M. (1993). Shadow and Substance: A Relational Perspective on Clinical Process. *Psychoanalytic Psychology*, *10*, 147-168.

Bromberg, P. M. (2000). Potholes on the Royal Road: Or Is It An Abyss. *Contemporary Psychoanalysis*, *36*, 5-28.

Bromberg, P. M. (2003). Something Wicked This Way Comes: Trauma, Dissociation and Conflict: The Space Where Psychoanalysis, Cognitive Science, and Neuroscience Overlap. *Psychoanalytic Psychology*, *20*, 558-574.

Clynes, M., & Panksepp, J. (1988). *Emotions and psychopathology*. New York, NY: Plenum Press.

Darwin, C. (2003). *On the origin of species*. NY, NY: Signet Classics

Davidson, R. J. (2004) Laterality and Emotion: An electrophysiological approach. *Handbook of Neuropsychology*, 419-441.

Davies, J. M., & Frawley, M. G. (1991). Dissociative Processes and Transference-Countertransference Paradigms in the Psychoanalytically Oriented Treatment of Adult Survivors of Childhood Sexual Abuse. In S. A. Mitchell & L. Aron (Eds.), *Relational psychoanalysis: the emergence of a tradition.* Hillsdale, NJ: Analytic Press.

Debellis, M., Keshavan, M., Clark, D., Casey. B., Gledd, J., Boring, A., Frustaci, K., Ryan, N. (1999). Developmental Traumatology Part II: Brain Development. Biological Psychiatry, 45, 1271 -1284.

Deutsch, J. A., & Deutsch, D. (1963). Attention: Some Theoretical Considerations. *Psychological Review, 70,* 80-90.

Diagnostic and statistical manual of mental disorders: DSM-IV-TR. (2000). Washington, DC: American Psychiatric Association.

Evans, F. B. (1996). *Harry Stack Sullivan interpersonal theory and psychotherapy*. London: Routledge.

Fairbairn, W. R. (1952). *Psychoanalytic studies of the personality*. London: Tavistock Publications.

Fairbairn, W. R. (1994). *Psychoanalytic studies of the personality*. London: Routledge.

Feiner, A. H. & Levinson, E.A. (1968 - 1969). The Compassionate Sacrifice: Exploration of a Metaphor. *Psychoanalytic Review, 55*, 552 - 573.

Fletcher, K., and Kabat-Zinn, J. (1995). Three-Year Follow-Up and Clinical Implications of a Mindfulness-Based Stress Reduction Intervention in the Treatment of Anxiety Disorders. General Hospital Psychiatry, 3, 192 - 200.

Freud, S. (1989). *The Freud reader* (P. Gay, Ed.). New York, NY: W.W. Norton.

Fromm, E. (1964). *The Heart of Man*. New York, NY: Harper and Row.

Goldson, E. (1989). Neurological Aspects of Failure to Thrive. *Developmental Medicine and Child Neurology, 31*, 821-826.

Greenberg, J. R., & Mitchell, S. A. (1983). *Object relations in psychoanalytic theory*. Cambridge, MA: Harvard University Press.

Guntrip, H. (1961). *Personality structure and human interaction; the developing synthesis of psycho-dynamic theory*. New York, NY: International Universities Press.

Guntrip, H. (1967). The Concept of Psychodynamic Science. *The International Journal of Psychoanalysis*, *48*, 32-43.

Guntrip, H. (1971). *Psychoanalytic theory, therapy, and the self*. New York, NY: Basic Books.

Guntrip, H. (2001). *Schizoid phenomena, object-relations, and the self*. Madison, CT: International Universities Press.

Harlow, H. F. (1959). Love in Infant Monkeys. *Scientific American*, *200*, 68-74.

Herman, J., & Van der Kolk, B. (1987). *Traumatic Antecedents of Patients with Borderline Personality Organization*. Washington, DC: American Psychiatric Press.

Herman, J. (1992). *Trauma and recovery*. New York, N.Y.: BasicBooks.

Hirsch, I. (1995). Changing Conceptions of Unconscious. *Contemporary Psychoanalysis*, *21*, 263-275.

Hirsch, I. (1997). The Widening Concept of Dissociation. *The Journal of The American Academy of Psychoanalysis and Dynamic Psychiatry*, *25*, 603-615.

Howell, E. F. (2002). Back to The States. *Psychoanalytic Dialogues*, *12*(6), 921-957.

Hull, A. (2002). Neuroimaging findings in post-traumatic stress disorder. *The British Journal of Psychiatry*, 102-110.

Hunter, R. (1973). Eyes of the World. Wake of the Flood. Record. San Francisco, CA: Grateful Dead Records.

Kazdin, A. E. (1998). *Research design in clinical psychology*. Boston, MA: Allyn and Bacon.

Kihlstrom, J. F., & Hoyt, I. P. (1990). Repression, dissociation, and hypnosis. In J. L. Singer (Ed.), Repression and dissociation: Implications for personality theory, psychopathology, and health (pp. 181-208). Chicago, IL.: University of Chicago Press.

Klein, J. (1987). *Our Need for Others and its Roots in Infancy*. London: Tavistock Publications.

Klein, M. (1930). The Importance of Symbol-Formation in the
Development of the Ego. *The International Journal of
Psychoanalysis*, *11*, 24-39.

Klein, M. (1932). The Psychoanalysis of Children. *The International
Psycho-Analytic Library*, *22*, 1-379.

Klein, M. (1935). A Contribution to the Psychogenesis of Manic-
Depressive States. *The International Journal of
Psychoanalysis*, *16*, 145-174.

Klein, M. (1952). The Origins of Transference. *The International
Journal of Psychoanalysis*, *33*, 433-438.

Klein, M. (1952). The Mutual Influences of the Ego and the Id.
Psychoanalytic Study of the Child, *7*, 51-52.

Klein, M. (1968). *Contributions to psycho-analysis, 1921-1945*.
London, England: Hogarth Press.

Klein, M. (1996). Notes on Some Schizoid Mechanisms. *Journal of
Psychotherapy Practice and Research*, *5*, 160-179.

Levine, P. A. (1997). *Waking the tiger: healing trauma : the innate
capacity to transform overwhelming experiences*. Berkeley,
CA: North Atlantic Books.

Likierman, M. (2001). *Melanie Klein: her work in context*. London, England: Continuum.

Linehan, M., Armstrong, H., Suare, A., Allmon, D., and Heard, H. (1991). Cognitive-Behavioral Treatment of Chronically Parasuicidal Borderline Patients. General Psychiatry, 48, 1060 - 1064.

Mancia, M. (2006). *Psychoanalysis and neuroscience*. Milan, Italy: Springer.

Mitchell, S. A. (1988). *Relational Concepts in Psychoanalysis: An Integration*. London: Tavistock Publications.

Mitchell, S. A., & Black, M. J. (1995). *Freud and beyond: a NY history of modern psychoanalytic thought*. New York, NY: BasicBooks.

Twemlow, S. W. & Gabbarg, G.O. (2004) *The Iatrogenics Handbook: A Critical Look at Research and Practice in the Helping Professions* (R. Morgan, Ed., 1st ed.). Toronto, Canada: IPI Pub.

Newell, W. H. (2001). A Theory of Interdisciplinary Studies. *A Theory of Interdisciplinary Studies, 19*, 1-25.

Parasuraman, R., & Rizzo, M. (2007). *Neuroergonomics the brain at work*. Oxford: Oxford University Press.

Pereira, F., & Scharff, D. E. (2002). *Fairbairn and relational theory*. London: Karnac.

Preston, A. (2007, September 26). How does short-term memory work in relation to long-term memory? *Scientific American*.

Putnam, F. W. (1989). *Diagnosis and treatment of multiple personality disorder*. New York, NY: Guilford Press.

Rogers, C. (1995). On Becoming a Person: A Therapist's View of Psychotherapy. New York, NY: Houghton Mifflin.

Russel, P. L. (1991). Trauma, Repetition, and Affect. *Presented at Massachusetts Institute for Psychoanalysis Symposium*.

Schachtel, E. (1959). *Metamorphosis*. New York, NY: Basic Books.

Searles, H. S. (1979). *Countertransference and Related Subjects*. New York, NY: International Universities Press.

Segal, J. (1992). *Melanie Klein*. London: Sage Publications.

Shyamalan, M. K. (Producer, Director). (2004). *The village* [Motion picture on DVD]. US: Touchstone Pictures.

Sommer-Anderson, F., & Gold, J. (2003). Trauma, Dissociation, and Conflict: The Space Where Neuroscience, Cognitive Science and Psychoanalysis Overlap,. *Psychoanalytic Psychology*, *20*, 536-541.

Stern, D. B. (1983). Unformulated Experience: From Familiar Chaos to Creative Disorder. *Contemporary Psychoanalysis*, *19*, 71-99.

Stern, D. B. (1995). *Pioneers of interpersonal psychoanalysis*. Hillsdale, NJ: Analytic Press.

Stern, D. B. (2003). The Fusion of Horizons: Dissociation, Enactment, and Understanding. *Psychoanalytic Dialogues*, *13*, 843-873.

Stern, D. B. (2004). The Eye Sees Itself: Dissociation, Enactment, and the Achievement of Conflict. *Contemporary Psychoanalysis*, *40*, 197-237.

Stolorow, R. D., Atwood, G. E., & Branchaft, B. (1994). *The Inter-Subjective perspective*. Northvale, NJ: J. Aronson.

Stolorow, R. D., Orange, D. M., & Atwood, G. E. (2001). World Horizons: A Post-Cartesian Alternative to the Freudian Unconscious. *Contemporary Psychoanalysis*, *37*, 43-61.

Sullivan, H. S. (1937). A Note on the Implications of Psychiatry, the Study of Interpersonal Relations, for Investigations in the

Social Sciences. *American Journal of Sociology, 42*(6), 848.

doi: 10.1086/217588.

Sullivan, H. S. (1953). *The interpersonal theory of psychiatry;.* New

York, NY: Norton.

Sullivan, H. S. (1954). *The psychiatric interview;.* New York, NY:

W.W. Norton.

Sullivan, H. S. (1956). *Clinical studies in psychiatry;.* New York,

NY: Norton.

Sun Tzu, (6th Century BC) *The Art of War.*

Thompson, C. (1950). *Psychoanalysis: evolution and development.*

New York, NY: Hermitage House.

Van Der Hart, O., Nijenhuis, E. R., & Steele, K. (2005).

Dissociation: An Insufficiently Recognized Major Feature of

Complex PTSD. *Journal of Traumatic Stress, 18*(5), 1-15.

Watson, S., Chilton, R., & Peter, W. (2006). Association Between

Childhood Trauma and Dissociation Among PAtients with

Borderline Personality Disorder. *The Australian and New

Zealand Journal of Psychiatry, 40,* 478-481.

Winnicott, D. W. (1960). The Theory of the Parent-Infant

    Relationship. *The International Journal of Psychoanalysis*,

    41, 585-595.

Winnicott, D. W. (1964). *Child the family and the outside world.*

    New York, NY: Penguin Books.

Winnicott, D. W. (1965). *The family and individual development.*

    New York, NY: Basic Books.

Winnicott, D. W. (1969). The Use of An Object. *The International*

    Journal of Psychoanalysis, *50*, 711-716.

Winnicott, D. W. (1988). *Human nature.* New York: Schocken

    Books.

www.ingramcontent.com/pod-product-compliance
Lightning Source LLC
Chambersburg PA
CBHW051342280526
45784CB00007B/2780